FIRED UP

NO NONSENSE BARBECUING

ROSS DOBSON

UP

MURDOCH BOOKS

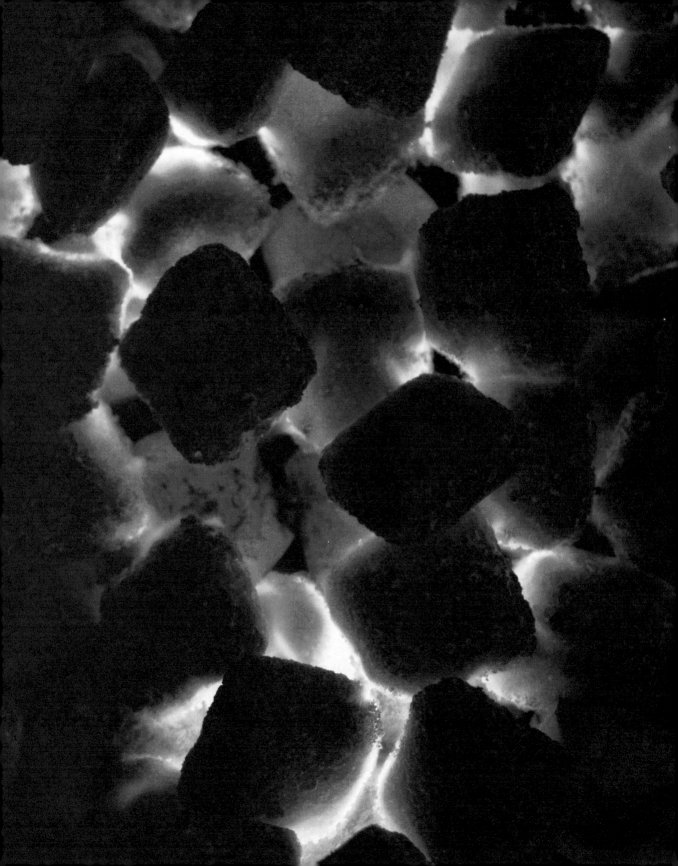

BARBECUING ESSENTIALS...7

BIRD...12
BEAST...64
FISH...152

SIDES...202

INDEX...220

BARBECUING ESSENTIALS

The more things change, the more they stay the same. In this crazy, fast-paced world I take great comfort in the very thought of a barbecue. And although your average barbecue may have evolved into a state-of-the-art, designed and intricate affair, in essence barbecuing is still just the same. If we so wish, barbecuing can be kept simple, and for me at least the satisfaction of handling a barbecue is one of life's pleasures that hasn't changed at all.

On this nostalgic note, there are many things from the 1980s—the Golden Age of the Barbecue—I wish I could forget and, for those of us who lived through it the first time around, some aspects of those days keep returning to annoy us like a slap in the face with a fish. In particular, there's one catchphrase from this time that established Australia on the barbecue map: 'Throw another shrimp on the barbie!' For those of you not familiar with this it was from a campaign aimed at luring tourists 'Down Under'—a cliché since hard to shake, I might add. But it was a campaign that was extremely successful. It evoked a sense of fun under the sun, of a casual, laid-back attitude and a celebration of the great outdoors. But to me the subtext was really about the unique Australian style of cooking and eating.

What and how we barbecue is indeed unique. I think we do, after all, prefer to throw a prawn (and it is a prawn NOT a shrimp) on the barbie rather than stand around for hours on end basting some huge unidentifiable piece of meat that will just end up shredded and in a sandwich. And this to me is the difference between how we barbecue and how those other great lovers of the barbecue, the North Americans, do it. While they are masters in the art of slow cooked, large cuts of meat basted, braised and sauced up until fork tender, the Australian way of barbecuing is really all about simplicity.

Of course, this doesn't deny the opportunity to marinate and baste. The flavours we use really do also reflect the range of ingredients we are afforded from our physical location on this planet, our climate and the diversity of cultures—taking advantage of all the flavours of Asia at our doorstep, embracing the exotic spices of the Middle East and Morocco, while continuing to have a deep love affair with the classic flavours of the Mediterranean. It's a global excursion—a multicultural journey in our very own backyard. All these wonderful flavours with a 'quick sticks' attitude of preparing and cooking—that is our idea of a barbecue.

For Australians the barbecue is also about getting out of the kitchen. I am not sure I see the point of saying something is barbecued if it has spent more time in the kitchen than outside on the barbecue. Forget the clichéd cultural connotations. Throwing a prawn on the barbie really is the essence of how and what we cook on the barbecue.

We all have our favourite animal to cook and you will find heaps of great recipes for your favourite—bird (chook, quail, duck, turkey), beast (cow, pig, lamb), or fish (anything aquatic). Whatever it is we cook, we fire it up, we do it fresh and we do it fast.

Let's not forget what it is all about. While I am the first to sing the praise of a great marinade or sauce, at the end of the day it is not about the barbecue sauce. It's about the barbecue.

Types of barbecues

Before talking about the actual types of barbecues, let's just establish exactly what it is a barbecue does.

A barbecue cooks food on a metal hotplate or grill, conducting the heat coming from underneath. The food can be cooked by either direct or indirect heat. For direct heat, think of a sausage. Not a very big piece of meat really and you cook it on the barbecue like you would in a frying pan—above the heat, turning often until evenly brown all over and cooked through. For indirect heat, think of a chicken. This is a rather dense piece of meat, bones included, and needs to be cooked on a barbecue which has a lid that can be closed. This creates an oven-type effect, so the heat circulates around the food, cooking it evenly to a golden crispy skin on the outside and, just like the sausage, cooked all the way through.

The most basic barbecue of course is an open fire. I think here of the type you see in camping grounds, where you are required to forage for your own wood, spark it up and get it going. It is fun but you wouldn't want to do this every day.

My first memory of a barbecue is a simple translation of this open-fire barbecue assembled in your own back yard—made of brick with a grill or hotplate suspended somewhere near the top and a place for wood to burn underneath. When these were around you asked a brickie to come over and actually build the thing for you.

The range of modern barbecues can only leave us feeling spoilt for choice, but they're more practical than the old-school, wood-burning, fixed barbecue.

A kettle barbecue sits on foldable or wheelable legs making it easy to get around. It has a rounded base (a bit like a big wok), which holds the hot coals, and you can cook the food over direct heat. A lid can be attached to cook the food on indirect heat, but for this the coals must be arranged in two rows on either side, leaving a space in the centre for a drip tray and for the heat to circulate evenly. If you can imagine that heat rises, kind of like steam in a shower that hits the ceiling, in a kettle barbecue it will bounce back down to heat the food.

Gas and electric barbecues are like cars. Some are like minis—light, small and easy to get around. Others are more like SUVs—big, showy and take up a lot of space. Whether a mini or an SUV, these barbecues are easy to fire up and the heat can be adjusted. Like the kettle barbecue, a gas barbecue with a hood will enable you to cook with indirect heat.

Electric barbecues can look and function just like a gas one except they will, of course, need to be plugged in somewhere, which can limit them. But the heat on these can be less intense than gas, coal or wood-fired barbecues.

Cooking on kettle and electric barbecues may need a little extra attention due to their heat variability and, with the kettle, its size. But fear not. A good barbecue has as much to do with an attentive cook as it does the barbecue. So do keep your eyes peeled making sure the food doesn't cook too quickly and burn, or cook too slowly and stew, defeating the whole purpose of a barbecue. And listen. You know the sound. Barbecued food ought gently sizzle which leads us to our third sense. Smell. We all know the smell of burnt food, so adjust your heat accordingly. When things look, smell and sound right they'll taste great, and this is the art of a great barbecue.

BIRD ESSENTIALS

I do wonder if chicken is overtaking red meat as the most popular barbecue item. Probably not, but it must be close! In the good old days, the roast chook was a rare treat, reserved for the family Sunday dinner. But no longer so. While once it was red meat and two veg, today the white meat of chicken has come to dominate our eating habits, and what better place to cook it than on the barbie.

Are you into breasts or thighs? I save chicken breast fillets for stir-fries, but if I do barbecue them I prefer a breast with the skin on, keeping the meat tender and juicy, mother nature's pouch ready to be filled with vinegar-spiked salsas, herb- and olive-flavoured butters or wrapped in bacon, barbecued to a smoky crisp. Thigh meat is my preferred bit of the chook with nice little pockets of fat that quickly render away on a hot grill, keeping the meat moist and tasty.

Don't think for a minute you need a fancy-pants barbecue set-up to cook a barbecued chicken, flavoured with just about whatever grabs you. All you need is a can of beer and a few easy-to-get spices and away you go. Chook loves full throttle Asian sauces, zesty and tangy lemon and lime, lemongrass, chilli, ginger and garlic. And these flavours don't just work for a chook. The sexy little quail loves them too. The classic duck recipe in this chapter is a beauty, a treat you won't just save for a special occasion. And all of the recipes here are great to serve up and enjoy in the great outdoors, especially if you are lucky enough to live in the southern hemisphere!

But remember, for a chicken to taste like a chicken it must have been able to live like one. This means lots of running around, just as nature intended, scratching, pecking and flapping their way through life. So do get your hands on a free-range or organic bird.

HONEY HOI SIN CHICKEN WINGS

SERVES 4

12 chicken wings

Hoi sin honey marinade
2 tablespoons light soy sauce
3 tablespoons hoi sin sauce
3 tablespoons tomato sauce (ketchup)
3 tablespoons honey
1 tablespoon sesame oil

Americans might call these devilled chicken wings, a favourite for both kiddies and adults alike as they are a sweet and sticky easy-to-eat treat, just as good as a cold snack as they are straight off the grill. The Asian sauces here are a must have, but this isn't too much of an ask as these ingredients can be picked up in just about any supermarket if you aren't near an Asian specialty store. They have good shelf life but once opened do keep them in the fridge. I say to marinate these overnight and if you do, remember to turn them often.

Cut the wing tips off the chicken wings, then cut the wings between the centre joint to give two pieces—one of them looking like a little drumstick. Put the chicken in a steamer lined with baking paper (a Chinese bamboo steamer is perfect), cover with the lid and sit the steamer over a saucepan of boiling water for 10 minutes. Remove the chicken wings and allow to cool.

Meanwhile, combine the hoi sin honey marinade ingredients.

Put the chicken wings in a non-metallic dish, pour over the marinade and toss to coat. Cover and put in the refrigerator for 3 hours or overnight, turning often.

Remove the chicken wings from the fridge 20 minutes before cooking.

Preheat the barbecue grill to low and brush with a little olive oil to grease. (The cooking is easy but you do have to keep your eyes and ears alert that the wings are gently sizzling.) Shake the excess marinade off the chicken into the dish, put the chicken wings on the grill, reserving the marinade, and cook for 2 minutes on each side until they begin to turn golden, then start to baste. Baste, turn and cook for 2 minutes, then repeat. Keep doing this for 10 to 12 minutes until the wings become deep reddish-brown, glazed and just starting to char.

BARBECUE CHICKEN WITH
GREEN OLIVE SALSA VERDE

SERVES 4

I use a procedure here called 'brining'. This is really nothing more than the most basic marinating method—soaking the meat in salt, sugar and spices—but the flavour is something else!

Cut the chickens in half through the breastbone, remove the cartilage and backbone, cut off the wing tips, then wash and pat dry with paper towel. Put the chickens in a snug-fitting non-metallic dish, cover and refrigerate.

Meanwhile, bring a large saucepan of water to the boil and add the table salt, sugar and bay leaves. Return to the boil, stir until the salt and sugar have dissolved, then remove from the heat and cool completely. Pour enough of the brine liquid over the chickens so they are well immersed and refrigerate for 3 to 6 hours or overnight.

For the salsa, tear the bread and put in a food processor with the olives, herbs, celery leaves, capers, garlic, anchovies and lemon juice. Pulse to combine, leaving the mixture a little chunky. Put into a bowl and stir through the olive oil, and add some freshly ground black pepper.

Remove the chickens from the brine and pat dry with paper towel. Put in a bowl and add the olive oil and lemon juice, rubbing the mixture all over the chickens. Season with sea salt and black pepper and set aside for 20 minutes.

Preheat the barbecue hotplate to low–medium. Put the chickens on the hotplate, skin side down. Put the lid on the barbecue and cook for 15 to 20 minutes, pressing down occasionally with a flat metal spatula, until the skin is dark golden and crispy. Turn the chicken over and cook for a further 15 minutes, until cooked through. You can test if it is ready by making a small, deep incision between the end of the drumstick and the breast. Any liquid that runs out should be clear, not bloody. Remove the chicken to a plate and lightly cover with foil for 10 minutes to rest.

You can serve half a chicken per person to feed four or cut each half into smaller pieces and arrange on a serving platter with the salsa verde spooned over and extra lemon wedges on the side.

2 x 1.25 kg (2 lb 12 oz) free-range chickens
140 g (5 oz/½ cup) table salt
60 g (2¼ oz/⅓ cup) brown sugar
3 bay leaves
3 tablespoons olive oil
3 tablespoons lemon juice

Green olive salsa verde
1 thick slice white bread, crusts removed
60 g (2¼ oz/½ cup) pitted green olives
large handful flat-leaf (Italian) parsley leaves, roughly chopped
1 large handful mint leaves, roughly chopped
1 large handful celery leaves, roughly chopped
1 tablespoon salted capers, well rinsed
2 garlic cloves, chopped
2 anchovy fillets
2 tablespoons lemon juice
3 tablespoons olive oil

THAI BARBECUED CHICKEN

Coriander and pepper rub

6 coriander roots and 4–5 cm (1¾–2 in) of the stem, washed and chopped
6 garlic cloves, chopped
½ teaspoon black peppercorns
½ teaspoon white peppercorns
3 tablespoons fish sauce
4 spring onions (scallions), chopped

1.5 kg (3 lb 5 oz) free-range chicken
coriander (cilantro) sprigs, to serve

If you look at the ingredients in the coriander rub you could be excused for thinking that it all sounds a bit full on. But that is the nature of Thai cooking. It is all in the balance. A good Thai meal is like a roller coaster of flavour in your mouth—challenging, scary to some and quite addictive. I actually like using this same rub on chicken thigh fillets, which have been gently pounded to flatten, and cooking them on a hot grill.

Put the coriander into a pestle with a generous pinch of sea salt. Pound for a couple of minutes until pulpy, then add the garlic. Pound again until the garlic is also pulpy, then add the remaining marinade ingredients. Pound until you have a chunky paste.

Put the chicken on a chopping board, breast side down. Use a sharp knife or cleaver to cut either side of the backbone and throw away. Open up the chicken to reveal the inside of the rib cage. Cut the chicken down the middle and carefully remove the cartilage. Turn over and cut several diagonal slashes across the skin of the chicken. Make the incisions deeper across the legs. Put into a flat non-metallic dish, skin side up, and rub the paste over the chicken. Cover and refrigerate for 3 to 6 hours.

Remove the chicken from the fridge 1 hour before cooking.

Preheat all the barbecue burners to low–medium. Drizzle a little olive oil on the hotplate to lightly grease. Put the chicken on the hotplate, skin side down, and cook for 10 minutes with the lid on. Reserve any marinade in the dish. The skin should really sizzle the entire cooking time. Spoon the reserved marinade over the chicken. Reduce the heat, turn the chicken over and cook for 15 to 20 minutes with the lid on, pressing down a few times on the legs with a flat metal spatula, until the chicken is cooked through. Put the chicken on a tray, cover with foil and leave to rest on a warm part of the barbecue (away from direct heat) for 10 minutes. Cut each half into several pieces and serve with coriander sprigs scattered over.

LEMON SOY ROAST CHICKEN

SERVES 4

I have tried to avoid recipes which require using barbecue equipment—built in rotisseries and the like. Although my barbecue does have one, I end up cooking a lot of chicken and meat on metal racks, either on a baking tray filled with hot water for big bits of meat or I sit the racks directly on the hotplate, which keeps the meat lifted up off the direct heat.

Put the soy, vinegar, lemon juice and sesame oil in a non-metallic dish large enough to put the chicken in. Put the chicken in the dish, breast side down, and rub over the marinade. Cover and refrigerate for 3 to 6 hours or overnight, turning often.

Remove the chicken from the marinade 1 hour before cooking and lightly pat dry with paper towel, pouring the marinade into a small saucepan. Put the garlic, spring onions, ginger and coriander roots in the cavity of the chicken and seal with half a lemon.

Preheat all the barbecue burners to low–medium, with the lid on creating an oven effect.

You will need a cooking or cake rack for this. Sit the chicken on the rack, breast side up. Rub the remaining lemon half over the chicken and sit on the hotplate. Put the lid on and cook for 30 minutes. Within a few minutes you should be able to hear the juices sizzling as they hit the hotplate. Turn the chicken over. It should be a dark caramel colour all over the underside. Cook with the breast side down for another 30 minutes. Sit the saucepan of the reserved marinade on the grill and begin to boil. Turn the chicken over once more and start to liberally baste with the now hot marinade. Cook the chicken for another 15 minutes with the lid on, basting every couple of minutes until the chicken is dark coloured all over. Test if the chicken is cooked by piercing the skin and flesh where the leg meets the thigh. If the juices are clear, it is ready. Remove the chicken to a plate and lightly cover with foil for 15 minutes before carving.

125 ml (4 fl oz/½ cup) light soy sauce
3 tablespoons Chinese black vinegar (or 2 tablespoons balsamic vinegar)
3 tablespoons lemon juice
1 tablespoon sesame oil
1.5 kg (3 lb 5 oz) free-range chicken
6 garlic cloves
2 spring onions (scallions)
6 thin slices ginger
4 coriander roots, washed
1 small lemon, cut in half

CHILLI CHICKEN BLT

2 large red chillies,
seeded and chopped
2 garlic cloves, chopped
handful flat-leaf (Italian)
parsley leaves, roughly
chopped
3 tablespoons
olive oil
2 large chicken breasts,
cut in half
4 rashers streaky bacon
4 soft bread rolls
mayonnaise
2 large handfuls baby rocket
(arugula)
2 tomatoes, finely sliced

This chicken is perfect as a spin on the old bacon, lettuce, tomato—BLT. Again, I am cooking the breast on a low–medium heat so the meat doesn't dry out too much, which chicken breast meat is prone to.

Put the chillies, garlic and parsley in a small food processor and whiz to combine. Add the oil and whiz until all the ingredients are finely chopped and flecked throughout the oil. Put the chicken in a snug-fitting non-metallic dish and pour over the marinade. Cover and refrigerate for 3 to 6 hours, or you could do this the day before.

Remove the chicken from the fridge 20 minutes before cooking. Put the halved chicken breasts on a chopping board and wrap each with a rasher of bacon.

Preheat the barbecue hotplate to low–medium and drizzle with a little olive oil to lightly grease. Put the chicken breasts on the hotplate and cook for 10 minutes. You may need to adjust the heat so the breasts gently sizzle the entire cooking time, watching that the bacon doesn't burn. Press down on the thickest part of the breast with a flat metal spatula a few times. Turn over and cook for another 10 minutes. Remove and rest on a plate for 5 minutes.

Serve the chicken as a BLT-type burger on the roll spread with mayonnaise and topped with rocket and tomato.

CHICKEN WITH TARRAGON, OLIVES AND GARLIC

SERVES 4

4 chicken breast fillets with wing attached and skin on
24 tarragon leaves
2 garlic cloves
2 tablespoons small black olives (in oil, not kalamata)

This is about as close as my barbecuing gets to fine dining. I feel like fresh tarragon has taken a back seat to the more trendy flavourings like coriander, Thai basil and lemongrass. But who can forget the first time they had a creamy tarragon chicken *vol-au-vent*? (If you haven't, dig out a '70s cookbook and give it a go.) The trick with tarragon is to use it sparingly and it does love being with chicken.

Carefully separate (but don't remove) the skin from the flesh of the chicken breasts, without tearing the skin, and set aside.

Put the tarragon leaves on a chopping board and roughly chop. Add the garlic and a good sprinkle of sea salt and chop the tarragon, garlic and salt together until they are finely chopped. Add the olives to the mix and finely chop. Spoon the mixture under the skin of the chicken breasts and rub evenly over the breast meat. Use a couple of toothpicks to secure the skin either side of the breast. (This will stop the skin from retracting too much when cooking.) Put on a plate, cover and refrigerate until needed.

Remove the chicken from the fridge 20 minutes before cooking.

Preheat the barbecue hotplate to medium. Drizzle a little olive oil over the skin of the chicken and sprinkle with some sea salt. Put on the hotplate and cook, skin side down, for 5 minutes, pressing down occasionally on the thickest part of the breast with a flat metal spatula. Reduce the heat to low, turn over and cook for a further 10 minutes, with the barbecue lid on. Again, press down a couple of times on the chicken with a spatula. Put the chicken on a heatproof plate, cover with foil and sit the plate on the hot barbecue lid for 5 minutes. Remove from the barbecue and let the chicken rest for a further 5 minutes before serving.

AMELIA'S QUAIL

Most of these are typical Asian flavourings so you may be wondering why the use of olive oil? That's what I asked myself one summer when a friend suggested I try these flavours as a marinade for tasty little quail. The fruity olive oil really enhances the simple yet distinctive flavours here. Nice one, Amelia.

8 quails
3 tablespoons olive oil
2 tablespoons light soy sauce
4 garlic cloves, roughly chopped
1 tablespoon lightly grated ginger

To prepare the quails, put on a chopping board, breast side up. Insert a heavy, sharp knife into the cavity. Firmly cut either side of the backbone, all the way through. Discard the backbone and spread the quail open on the chopping board with the skin side up. Press down firmly to flatten the bird. Cut off each of the wing tips and throw away. Cut in half through the breastbone. Now cut each of the halves in half again, so the legs and thighs are separated from the breast. Wash and pat dry with paper towel and put the quails in a snug-fitting non-metallic dish.

Combine the other ingredients in a bowl and pour over the quail, tossing the quail pieces around so they are evenly coated in the marinade. Cover and set aside for 30 minutes or put in the refrigerator for 3 to 6 hours, turning them often. If you do refrigerate the quails just remember to take them out of the fridge 1 hour before cooking. The cooking time is short so you don't want them to still be cold in the centre.

Preheat the barbecue hotplate to medium. Shake any excess marinade off the quail and reserve for later use. Put the quail on the hotplate and cook, skin side down for 2 minutes. Reduce the heat to low and cook for another 4 minutes, pressing down occasionally with a flat metal spatula on the thicker breast pieces. The skin should be golden brown. Turn the quail over, cover the barbecue with the lid and cook for 5 minutes, again pressing down a couple of times on the thicker pieces. Working quickly, stir the reserved marinade and pour evenly over the quail, turn the birds a couple of times to coat in the sauce. Remove to a platter, cover lightly with foil and let the quails rest for 5 minutes before serving.

LEMON THYME CHICKEN WINGS

12 chicken wings

Lemon thyme marinade
3 tablespoons olive oil
2–3 tablespoons lemon juice
3 garlic cloves, crushed
¼ teaspoon chilli powder
6 lemon thyme sprigs
extra chilli powder,
to serve

These are a favourite. The marinade timing is the big thing here. Basically, the longer the better. The cooking tip here was serendipitous. Actually, the first time I made it I forgot to preheat the barbecue, so I started putting the chicken on a cold hotplate. I quickly noticed a lack of sizzle (and of course heat) but I continued to arrange the chicken on the hotplate then turned on the heat. It worked a treat with these but I wouldn't try it with other bits of meat or seafood.

Cut the wing tips off the chicken wings, then cut the wings between the centre joint to give two pieces and put in a snug-fitting non-metallic dish. Mix together the marinade ingredients, pour over the chicken and toss to coat. Cover and put in the refrigerator for 3 hours or overnight, turning often.

Remove the chicken from the fridge 20 minutes before cooking.

Make sure your barbecue hotplate is clean but don't preheat. Put the wings and the lemon thyme sprigs on the hotplate then turn the heat on to medium. Reserve any marinade. Keep your ears tuned and when the chicken skin starts to gently sizzle, begin timing. Put the lid on and cook for 10 minutes, basting occasionally—but don't be tempted to turn the chicken too early. Turn and cook for another 5 minutes and continue to baste, until the chicken is crispy and golden.

Remove the chicken wings to a plate, lightly cover with foil and let them sit for a few minutes. You can add some sea salt here and some extra fresh lemon juice if that's your thing. Serve sprinkled with extra chilli powder to taste.

BEER-CAN ROASTED CHICKEN

SERVES 4

2 x 1.5 kg (3 lb 5 oz)
free-range chickens
1 lemon
1 tablespoon
Cajun seasoning
1 tablespoon olive oil
1 tablespoon finely chopped
tarragon
1 tablespoon finely chopped
flat-leaf (Italian) parsley
2 tablespoons finely
chopped coriander (cilantro)
2 tablespoons lemon juice
2 x 375 ml (13 fl oz/
1½ cups) can of beer
coriander, extra, roughly
chopped
1 lemon (or lime),
cut in half

In cooking this you could be excused for thinking you have reinvented the wheel. You see, there has always been a problem in roasting a chicken on the barbecue if you don't have a fancy-pants rotisserie. If you do, good on you! But if you don't, then what do you do?

Well, there is something right under our noses at a barbecue that can solve this problem—a half-full can of beer. The obvious advantages of beer-can chook are twofold—sitting the chicken on the beer can keeps the bird up off the hotplate and meanwhile the beer itself slowly boils, steaming the inside of the chicken. The result is a perfectly roasted, moist and tender chicken.

Wash the chickens inside and out with cold water, pat dry with paper towel, then rub all over with lemon.

Combine the Cajun seasoning in a little bowl with the oil and herbs to form a paste. Brush over the skin of the birds, then sprinkle with a good amount of sea salt.

Preheat the barbecue to hot. If you have an average three-burner barbecue (one hotplate and two grills, or vice versa) put them all on as you really want to crank the heat up so it acts like an oven. And you will need a barbecue with a lid for this.

Drink some of the beer, not too much, no more than a couple of big sips. Now sit the chickens on the beer cans so the cans fit snugly in the chickens' cloaca (technical term for the cavity, AKA 'the clacka').

Sit the cans on the barbecue, making sure the end of the drumsticks are at the same level as the bottom of the beer cans (so they sit balanced on the hotplate). Close the lid and cook for 1 hour. (If the chooks are a bit bigger, say 1.8 kg/4 lb, give them 10 more minutes.) Test if the chickens are cooked by piercing the skin and flesh where the leg meets the thigh. If the juices are clear, they are ready. Remove the chickens to a plate and lightly cover with foil for 15 minutes before cutting each into 10 to 12 small pieces. Sprinkle over the extra coriander and serve with the fresh lemon or lime to squeeze over.

This is great served with the home-made sweet chilli sauce (page 212).

CHILLI CARAMEL CHICKEN

SERVES 4

Chilli caramel baste
3 tablespoons rice vinegar
3 tablespoons
light soy sauce
1 tablespoon fish sauce
2 tablespoons white sugar
1 teaspoon dried
chilli flakes
2 garlic cloves,
finely chopped

4 chicken breast fillets with
wing attached, with skin on
1 teaspoon white pepper

When you use sugar or sweet sauces and honeys in a marinade you have to watch out that it doesn't burn the meat when cooking. I try to avoid this by using any overly sweet concoction as a baste, not a marinade. So basically, cook the meat first then patiently baste in any sweet sauce for the desired result. This recipe calls for chicken breast fillets with skin on, but skinless breast fillets can also be used.

Combine the basting ingredients in a small jug or bowl and set aside.

Remove the chicken from the fridge 20 minutes before cooking and sprinkle some sea salt and white pepper over the skin.

Preheat the barbecue hotplate to high and drizzle with a little vegetable oil to grease. Put the chicken on the hotplate and cook, skin side down, for 4 to 5 minutes, until the skin begins to turn golden and crispy. Turn over and cook for another 3 minutes.

Turn the barbecue down to medium. Baste the skin side of the chicken, turn over and cook for 1 minute. Repeat this process until all the baste has been used up and the chicken has a dark caramel glaze all over—this should take a further 8 to 10 minutes. Remove to a plate, lightly cover with foil and allow to rest for 5 minutes before serving.

LEMONGRASS
AND LIME LEAF CHICKEN

You may have guessed that lemongrass is a grass. The top, green part is more fibrous and less flavoursome, so use the soft white part of the grass, close to the bottom for the best results. If you live somewhere temperate it is easy to grow lemongrass and is much better when picked and used fresh. This is something I often serve in summer, with some boiled rice and greens, and some Chinese chilli sauce on the side.

For the marinade, put the lemongrass, makrut leaves, garlic, ginger and spring onions in a food processor and whiz until the mixture looks like a fibrous and chunky paste. Put in a bowl and stir through the oil and fish sauce.

Put the chicken in a snug-fitting non-metallic dish. (Chicken thighs often have a little fat which is okay to leave on. You can trim the fat if you really want to, but they are cooked so well here that the fat will only render off and give a little extra flavour, and keep the meat moist as it cooks.) Pour on the marinade and rub all over the chicken. Cover and refrigerate for 3 to 6 hours or overnight, turning often.

Remove the chicken from the fridge 20 minutes before cooking.

Preheat the barbecue grill to high. When it is hot, brush just a little vegetable oil onto the grill. Put the chicken on the grill and cook for 5 minutes, pressing down occasionally on the thickest part of the thigh with a flat metal spatula. This is the part that is often left under-cooked, which is what you don't want with chook. There should be a golden crust formed on the cooked side. Turn the chicken over and cook for another 5 minutes. Remove to a plate, lightly cover with foil and allow to rest for 5 minutes before eating.

Lemongrass and lime leaf marinade
2 lemongrass stalks, white part only, finely sliced
4 small makrut (kaffir lime) lime leaves, very finely shredded
3 garlic cloves, chopped
1 tablespoon grated ginger
2 spring onions (scallions), chopped
1 tablespoon olive oil
1 tablespoon fish sauce

8 chicken thigh fillets

TERIYAKI AND MUSTARD
CHICKEN

The Japanese are one of the masters of really tasty grilled food. Yet, the flavourings are pretty much always the same, just used in different ratios. The beer is not a traditional Japanese marinade ingredient, but I couldn't resist using it to add extra flavour to my favourite cut of chicken, the tender thigh.

Combine the teriyaki and beer sauce ingredients in a small bowl and stir until the sugar has dissolved. Put the chicken fillets in a flat non-metallic dish and pour over the marinade. Cover and refrigerate for no more than 3 hours, turning the chicken often.

Remove the chicken from the fridge 20 minutes before cooking.

Preheat the barbecue grill to medium and brush with a little vegetable oil to grease. Put the chicken thighs on the grill, reserving the marinade, and cook for 5 minutes, then turn over and cook for a further 3 minutes. Now start basting with the teriyaki and beer sauce, turning the chicken over every minute. Continue this process for about 4 minutes, until the edges of the thighs are starting to look slightly charred and the rest of the chicken is a dark amber, golden colour. Remove to a plate, lightly cover with foil and allow to rest for 5 minutes before eating.

Teriyaki and beer sauce
3 tablespoons beer (a light ale is good here, preferably Japanese)
3 tablespoons Japanese soy sauce
1 tablespoon sugar
1 teaspoon mustard powder

8 chicken thigh fillets

VERDANT CHOOK

Herb marinade
3 tablespoons olive oil
2 garlic cloves
4 anchovies plus
2 teaspoons oil from the jar
2 tablespoons salted capers,
well rinsed
1 tablespoon Dijon mustard
handful parsley leaves
handful basil leaves
handful mint leaves
2 tablespoons lemon juice

4 chicken breast fillets with
wing attached and skin on

Similar to a salsa verde, but without the bread. All the fresh herbs make this chicken dish a very fresh-tasting number, and the versatile sauce could be served up with any cuts of simple barbecued chicken or lamb.

Put all the marinade ingredients in a food processor and process for just a few seconds until you have a herby, green and chunky sauce. Add some freshly ground black pepper to taste.

Carefully separate (but don't remove) the skin from the flesh of the chicken breasts, without tearing the skin, and put in a snug-fitting non-metallic dish. Rub the marinade under the skin, then cover and refrigerate for at least 3 hours or overnight.

Remove the chicken from the fridge 20 minutes before cooking.

Preheat the barbecue hotplate to medium. Put the chicken on the hotplate, skin side down, and cook for 5 minutes, pressing down occasionally on the thickest part of the breast with a flat metal spatula. When the skin develops a golden crust turn the chicken over, turn the heat down to low and cook for another 10 minutes, again pressing down a few times on the thickest part. Make sure the chicken has a low and even sizzle for the cooking time—you may need to adjust the heat on your barbecue. Remove to a plate and lightly cover with foil for 10 minutes before serving.

Now, if you happen to have any left over, or maybe cook extra, then this chicken is ideal eaten cold, thinly sliced and added to a salad the next day.

QUAILS WITH PEANUTS AND THAI HERBS

SERVES 4

If you haven't noticed I am a big fan of Asian flavours, and I find that the fresh Thai ingredients work well in barbecuing. These flavours also very much typify modern Australian cooking. This recipe uses lots of exotic herbs, that thrive in our climate, combined with Thai staples that can be bought easily at any local Asian specialty stores and most supermarkets.

For the Thai pesto, put all the ingredients in a food processor and whiz to a chunky paste. Put in a container and refrigerate until ready to use.

To prepare the quails, put one on a chopping board, breast side up. Hold the bird with one hand and insert a heavy, sharp knife into the cavity, firmly cutting either side of the backbone all the way through. Throw the backbone away and spread the quail open on the chopping board with the skin side up. Press firmly down on the breast with the palm of your hand to flatten the bird. Repeat with the other quails so you have eight butterflied quail. Wash the quail and pat dry. Now gently separate the skin from the flesh, being careful not to tear the skin. Reserve 60 g (2¼ oz/¼ cup) of the pesto and put aside. Spoon some of the remaining pesto under the skin and gently spread over the breast and as far down towards the leg as you can, without tearing the skin. Put the quail on a baking tray lined with baking paper, cover and refrigerate until needed.

Remove the quail from the fridge, squeeze the lime over the skin of each and set aside for 20 minutes.

Preheat the barbecue hotplate to medium and drizzle with a little olive oil to grease. Put the quail on the hotplate and cook, skin side down, for 5 minutes with the lid on until the skin is crispy and dark golden. Reduce the heat to low, turn the quail over and cook for another 10 minutes. Remove to a plate, lightly cover with foil and rest for 5 minutes. Serve with the reserved pesto spooned over with coriander and white pepper.

Thai pesto
40 g (1½ oz/¼ cup) crushed peanuts
2 garlic cloves, chopped
¼ teaspoon white pepper
1 large green chilli, chopped
1 small bunch Thai basil leaves
1 small bunch coriander (cilantro), leaves only
1 small bunch mint leaves, roughly chopped
1 tablespoon fish sauce
1 teaspoon sugar
1 tablespoon lime juice
1 tablespoon olive oil

8 jumbo quails, about 200 g (7 oz) each
1 lime, cut in half
handful coriander, roughly chopped
1 teaspoon white pepper, extra

BLACKENED BIRD

SERVES 4

Cajun rub
2 tablespoons smoked paprika
1 teaspoon dried oregano
1 teaspoon dried thyme
¼ teaspoon cayenne pepper
2 teaspoons sea salt flakes
2 garlic cloves, crushed
2 tablespoons light olive oil

2 x small spatchcock, about 500 g (1 lb 2 oz) each

This is Cajun cooking at its finest, nothing more or less. Let the classic spice rub weave it's spell as it defies the sum of its parts. On their own these are really full throttle flavours—but combined they become voodoo magic!

Combine the spice rub ingredients in a small bowl and set aside.

Cut the spatchcock in half through the breastbone to give four portions of bird. Remove the cartilage in the breastbone and cut off the wing tips. Wash and pat dry with paper towel.

Rub the spice blend all over the birds and put in a snug-fitting non-metallic dish. Cover and refrigerate for at least 3 hours or overnight if you like.

Preheat the barbecue hotplate to medium. Sit a rack on the hotplate—this will keep the birds lifted up from the direct heat, preventing them from burning.

Sit the birds on the rack, skin side up. Cover the barbecue with the lid and cook for 35 to 40 minutes. They should be darkened with a reddish tone from the paprika. Remove to a plate and gently cover with foil for about 15 minutes. Not too tight. You don't want them to sweat and the skin to lose its crispiness under there. Serve whole.

Next time: Cut a large chicken, about 1.8 kg (4 lb), in half like the smaller birds and then cut the halves across to give four portions from the one large chicken. Rub with the spice blend and refrigerate overnight. Cook on a hotplate preheated to medium for 15 minutes skin side down, turn over and cook for another 15 to 20 minutes, until the juices are no longer pink when pierced with a skewer.

DUCK WITH SAFFRON RICE STUFFING AND ROASTED VEGGIES

serves 4

2.5 kg (5 lb 8 oz)
roasting duck
2 tablespoons sea salt
8 small new potatoes
2 carrots, cut into
long pieces
2 parsnips, cut into
long pieces

Saffron rice stuffing
1 small white onion,
finely chopped
1 garlic clove, chopped
½ teaspoon saffron threads
2 bay leaves
100 g (3½ oz/½ cup)
long-grain rice
1 teaspoon ground ginger
250 ml (9 fl oz/1 cup)
chicken stock

Duck is a funny one. To be honest, there was a time when I was a little reluctant to cook with it as many recipes seemed like too much work for too little pleasure. Save confit for eating out. Then two things happened. Duck became less expensive and I threw away the recipe book for cooking it. When I mastered a simple roast duck in my oven it then became all too easy to take it outside to the barbecue and with all that hot fat around, the outside seems like the best place. Up there with the glazed ham, this could be served up as a regular Christmas treat. The veggies are a great filler, without them I could eat a half duck to myself.

Trim the excess fat from around the duck cavity and cut off the neck, leaving 2 to 3 cm (¾ to 1¼ in) of neck intact. Wash the duck thoroughly and pat dry with paper towel, inside and out. Set aside for 1 hour.

For the stuffing, put the onion, garlic, saffron and bay leaves in a small saucepan with 125 ml (4½ fl oz/½ cup) of water and cook on high heat for 5 minutes, so the onions soften and the water has evaporated. Add the rice and ginger and cook for 1 minute, stirring so the rice looks shiny. Add the chicken stock, bring to the boil then cover tightly. Cook on low heat for 10 minutes, so the rice is partially cooked and the stock is absorbed.

Preheat all the barbecue burners to low, with the lid on. This will create a hot oven type effect in which to roast the duck. Loosen the skin and pierce with a skewer all over. This will help the fat drain out as it cooks. Spoon the rice stuffing into the cavity and seal the cavity with a skewer. Rub the sea salt all over the duck and sit on a cooking rack over a deep baking tray.

Sit the tray on the hotplate of the barbecue, cover with the lid and cook for 1 hour. Check after 30 minutes. The skin will have just started to shrink and look slightly golden. If the side of the duck facing the grills is cooking quicker you may need to turn off the grill burner, or one of them, as heat flows vary from barbecue to barbecue.

Carefully lift the rack to one side and pour off all the fat, and as much sediment as possible, from the roasting tray into a heatproof dish. Arrange the vegetables in a single layer on the roasting tray then spoon over 2 tablespoons of the hot duck fat. Sit the rack back on the tray and spoon 1 tablespoon of the fat over the duck breasts. Cover and cook for 30 minutes.

Again, remove the duck to one side. Carefully pour off any excess fat in the roasting tray, leaving about 2 tablespoons. Turn the vegetables over and return the rack to the tray. Baste the duck with 1 tablespoon of the fat, cover and cook for another 30 minutes.

By this time the duck will be dark golden and the vegetables cooked. Remove the veggies to a heatproof plate and cover lightly with foil. Leaving the duck over the roasting tray, turn all the barbecue burners to high, cover and cook for 10 to 15 minutes, so the duck skin is crispy and dark golden all over. Sit the tray of veggies on the hot hood of the barbecue to keep warm.

Remove the duck, cover lightly with foil to keep warm and rest for 15 minutes. Cut the duck into quarters and serve with the stuffing and roasted veggies.

LEMON CHICKEN, FETA AND HERB INVOLTINI

SERVES 4

4 large chicken thigh fillets
35 g (1¼ oz/¼ cup) soft feta cheese (marinated or Persian feta)
4 short rosemary sprigs
2 tablespoons olive oil
2 tablespoons lemon juice
handful flat-leaf (Italian) parsley leaves, roughly chopped
2 tablespoons chopped oregano leaves

This is an Italian thing—rolling a flattened piece of meat, usually veal, into a log and flavouring it with anything you like, really. I had to have an excuse to include soft marinated feta in a recipe in this book, so here it is. These *involtini* are thick buggers, so don't rush them, let them sizzle gently and slowly and you will be rewarded.

Put a chicken thigh between two layers of plastic food wrap and gently pound so it is an even thickness all over, about 5 mm (¼ in). Repeat with the remaining chicken thighs. Spread 1 tablespoon of feta over each flattened thigh and put a sprig of rosemary across. Sprinkle a little sea salt (but not too much as the feta could be salty enough) and some freshly ground black pepper over the meat and gently roll up the thigh, from one short end to the next, enclosing the feta and rosemary so it sticks out either end. Tie the *involtini* with kitchen string and put in a non-metallic dish. Repeat to make four *involtini*. Combine the olive oil, lemon juice and remaining herbs in a bowl and pour over the chicken. Cover and refrigerate for at least 3 hours.

Remove the *involtini* from the fridge 20 minutes before cooking.

Preheat the barbecue hotplate to low. Put the *involtini* on the hotplate and cook for about 16 to 18 minutes, turning often so they sizzle the whole time and are golden brown all over. Put the *involtini* on a heatproof plate, cover with foil and sit on the lid of the warm barbecue for 10 minutes to rest before serving.

CHIMICHURRI CHOOK

This is the stuff of folklore and urban myth—researching the famous Argentinean/Uruguayan steak condiment I've come across many tales. I do like the one ditty that claims for the sauce to be authentic the meat you marinate it in must taste like it has been dragged through the garden! Another tale goes, it was named after an Irishman by the name of Jimmy Curry (say it quickly enough, after a few drinks on a warm day, and you may end up saying something like chimichurri). But this tale sounds like a bit of a stretch.

For the chimichurri, put the garlic and sea salt in a pestle and pound to a chunky paste. Add the herbs, spices and olive oil and pound to combine then stir through the red wine vinegar. Set aside for the flavours to develop. Soak some bamboo skewers.

Cut each chicken breast into four to six large chunky pieces and put in a non-metallic dish. Pour over the chimichurri marinade and toss to coat the chicken pieces. Cover and refrigerate for no longer than 3 hours, otherwise the vinegar will start to 'cook' the chicken.

Remove the chicken from the fridge 20 minutes before cooking and thread 3 to 4 pieces of meat onto the skewers. Put the skewers on a plate and reserve the marinade.

Preheat the barbecue hotplate to medium. Put the chicken skewers on the hotplate and cook for about 12 minutes, brushing over any of the marinade and turning so each side cooks for 3 minutes. When the skewers are golden brown, remove, squeeze over the fresh lemon, season to taste and serve.

Chimichurri
2 garlic cloves, coarsely chopped
½ teaspoon sea salt
small handful flat-leaf (Italian) parsley, coarsely chopped
1 tablespoon chopped oregano leaves
small handful coriander (cilantro) leaves and some stems, coarsely chopped
¼ teaspoon cayenne pepper, or a big pinch
¼ teaspoon Hungarian paprika
3 tablespoons olive oil
3 tablespoons red wine vinegar

4 chicken breast fillets, with skin on
1 lemon, cut in half

GREEN CURRY CHICKEN

Green curry paste
1 teaspoon coriander seeds
1 teaspoon cumin seeds
1 teaspoon white
peppercorns
2 large green chillies,
seeded and chopped
1 lemongrass stalk, chopped
2 garlic cloves, chopped
3 spring onions (scallions),
roughly chopped
4 small makrut (kaffir lime)
leaves, shredded
1 tablespoon grated ginger
4 coriander roots
4–5 cm (1¾–2 in) coriander
(cilantro) stem, washed
and chopped
1 tablespoon fish sauce
1 tablespoon sugar
3 tablespoons coconut
cream

8 chicken leg quarters

This really isn't an authentic 'curry' but has all the great flavours of a Thai green curry. Again, when cooking chicken on the bone do be patient and remove it from the fridge about 20 minutes before cooking. I raise an eyebrow, and so should you, if you see a recipe asking for chicken on the bone to be cooked for a mere 5 minutes each side. It will be raw and pink—bloody chicken is not a good thing.

Put the coriander and cumin seeds and peppercorns in a small frying pan over high heat, shaking the pan, until they start to smoke and darken. Remove from the pan and allow to cool. Put them in a small food processor or spice mill and grind. Add the remaining curry paste ingredients and process, stopping and starting the food processor a few times, scraping down the sides of the bowl until you have a chunky, pale green paste.

Cut the chicken between the drumstick and thigh joint. Gently separate the skin from the meat and put the chicken pieces in a non-metallic dish. Rub the paste all over the chicken pieces, including under the skin. Cover and refrigerate for 3 to 6 hours or overnight, but remember to remove from the fridge 20 minutes before cooking.

Preheat the barbecue hotplate to low and drizzle with a little vegetable oil to lightly grease. Put the chicken on the hotplate, and cook, skin side down, for 10 minutes with the lid on, pressing down occasionally with a flat metal spatula. They should gently sizzle until the spices cook, turning the skin into a golden crust. Turn over and continue to cook for 15 minutes, with the lid on. Remove the chicken to a heatproof serving plate, lightly cover with foil and sit the chicken on the warm barbecue lid for 10 minutes to rest.

SWEET CHILLI AND GINGER CHICKEN

In recent years sweet chilli sauce has come to sit proudly next to tomato sauce as a kitchen staple, a true sign of the culinary times. I personally find it too sweet and sticky as a sauce, but these qualities make it perfect as a sweet marinade base—with all its hidden ingredients—making cooking easy.

Put a chicken thigh between two layers of plastic food wrap and gently pound so it is an even thickness all over, about 5 mm (¼ in). I like to leave the little fat that is on the thigh on—it will keep the meat really moist while it cooks. Repeat with the remaining chicken thighs.

Put the chicken in a flat non-metallic dish. Combine the marinade ingredients in a bowl, pour over the chicken and rub all over the meat. Cover and refrigerate for 3 to 6 hours.

Remove the chicken from the fridge 20 minutes before cooking.

Preheat the barbecue grill to high and brush with a little vegetable oil to grease. Put the chicken on the grill and cook for 2 minutes, gently pressing down occasionally with a flat metal spatula. Turn over and cook for another 2 minutes, again pressing down on the meat. Remove to a platter, lightly cover with foil and leave to stand for 5 minutes before serving.

8 chicken thigh fillets

Sweet chilli marinade
150 g (5½ oz/½ cup) Thai sweet chilli sauce
2 tablespoons Chinese rice wine (or dry white wine)
1 tablespoon fish sauce
1 tablespoon finely grated ginger
1 small bunch coriander (cilantro), chopped

HARISSA CHICKEN

Harissa
10–12 dried chillies
4 large red chillies, seeded
and chopped
3 garlic cloves, chopped
1 teaspoon caraway seeds
3 tablespoons olive oil

12 chicken drumsticks
handful each of coriander
(cilantro) leaves and flat-leaf
(Italian) parsley, coarsely
chopped

Harissa takes many forms. It is a spice blend originating in Africa and you may have seen it in a paste or sauce, flavoured intensely with chillies and made wet and saucy with a mixture of fresh chillies and red peppers. Garlic and other combinations of spices are thrown in.

Seed the dried chillies if you want less heat (I don't generally), then put them in a heatproof bowl and cover with boiling water. Soak the chillies for 30 minutes, drain and roughly chop. Put the chopped chillies into a spice mill or pestle with the fresh chillies, garlic, caraway seeds, olive oil and a generous pinch of sea salt, and grind until you have a rough paste.

Cut a couple of deep incisions across the skin side of the drumsticks and put them in a snug-fitting non-metallic dish. Pour over the harissa and stir well so the drumsticks are evenly covered. Cover and refrigerate for 3 to 6 hours or overnight if you have the time.

Preheat the barbecue hotplate to medium.

You will notice your average chicken leg is shaped roughly like an oval sphere but with two wider sides and two more-narrow sides. Put the chicken on the hotplate, on one of the broader skin sides, and let them gently sizzle without turning or moving for 8 minutes. Turn over and cook for another 8 minutes, again without turning or moving the chicken. Now turn and cook on one narrow side for 3 minutes, then finally turn and cook on the other narrow side for a further 3 minutes. The chicken should be a golden rusty brown colour. Put the chicken in a large bowl, cover with foil and allow to rest for 5 minutes. Add the chopped herbs to the bowl, toss to coat the chicken and serve.

MEXICAN PESTO CHICKEN

SERVES 4

Chilli pesto
2 large green chillies
25 g (1 oz/¼ cup) pepitas
(pumpkin seeds), lightly
toasted until golden
40 g (1½ oz/¼ cup) pine
nuts, lightly toasted
until golden
1 small bunch coriander
(cilantro), chopped
1 tablespoon olive oil
2 tablespoons lime juice
2 tablespoons finely grated
parmesan cheese

1.6 kg (3 lb 8 oz)
free-range chicken
1 lime, cut in half

Pesto or the French 'pistou' is a classic side to grilled chicken and fish. This Mexican-style pesto includes chilli for a bit of kick.

Put the chillies over a naked gas flame, or on the grill of your barbecue, and cook until charred all over, turning often with tongs. Remove to a plastic bag to help them sweat and allow to cool. Roughly peel the chillies then put in a food processor with the pumpkin seeds, pine nuts, coriander, olive oil and lime juice. Process to a chunky paste. Put in a non-metallic bowl, stir through the parmesan and set aside. This can be made the day before if you like.

Cut the chicken in half through the breastbone, remove the cartilage and backbone, cut off the wing tips, then wash and pat dry with paper towel. Gently separate the skin from the meat, being careful not to tear the skin. Spoon the pesto under the skin, smothering it over the leg and breast meat. Secure the meat to the skin using toothpicks. (This will stop the skin from pulling back when cooking.) Rub the lime halves over the skin of the chicken, squeezing the lime as you do so. Cover and set aside at room temperature for 20 minutes.

Preheat the barbecue hotplate to high and the grill to low–medium. You will need a cooking or cake rack for this. Drizzle a little vegetable oil over the hotplate to grease. Put the chicken on the hotplate and cook, skin side down, for 3 minutes with the lid on until the skin is golden brown and crispy. Now put the chicken, skin side up, on the rack and sit the rack over the grill so the chicken is not sitting directly on the grill. Close the lid and cook for another 20 minutes. The skin of the chicken will look split in some places and the tasty pesto will have oozed out a bit. Test if the chicken is cooked by piercing the skin and flesh where the leg meets the thigh. If the juices are clear, it is ready. Remove the chicken to a plate and lightly cover with foil for 10 minutes to rest. To serve, cut each half in half again to make four pieces.

FINO SHERRY CHICKEN

Fino is a dry sweet sherry used in this simple marinade. Serve this chicken with any potato side (wedges, potato salad or baked) and coleslaw.

Combine the sherry, garlic and bay leaves in a bowl. Put the chicken pieces in a single layer in a snug-fitting non-metallic dish and pour over the marinade mixture. Cover and refrigerate overnight, turning often.

Remove the chicken from the fridge 20 minutes before cooking. Take the chicken out of the marinade, pat dry with paper towel and put the marinade in a small saucepan.

Preheat the barbecue hotplate to low and drizzle with a little olive oil to grease. Season the skin of the chicken with sea salt and freshly ground black pepper and cook for 5 minutes on each side, until golden brown.

Reduce the heat to low and add the garlic and bay leaves to the hotplate. Sit the saucepan with the marinade on a warm part of the barbecue and start to baste the chicken with it. When all the pieces have been basted, turn over and cook for 2 minutes. Repeat until the chicken is the colour of dark toffee and all the basting liquid has been used. This should take about 15 minutes. Turn the barbecue off. Wrap the pieces of chicken in cooking foil and sit on top of the hot lid of the barbecue for 10 minutes. Remove and allow to rest for another 10 minutes before unwrapping and serving.

250 ml (9 fl oz/1 cup) fino sherry
1 garlic bulb, separated, unpeeled
6 bay leaves
1.8 kg (4 lb) free-range chicken, cut into 8 portions

TURKEY BREAST
WITH HERBED CRUST

I use the technique of brining here, which gives the bird more flavour. But if you don't have the time to brine the turkey, don't worry. The herb crust is intensely flavoured with sage and lemon juice but the subtle white meat of turkey does need a good kick-start. Again, do be patient when cooking this bird as the turkey breast really is a big, dense piece of meat that takes time to cook all the way through.

Put the whole turkey breast in a non-metallic dish, cover and refrigerate. Bring 3 litres (105 fl oz/12 cups) of water to the boil and add the salt and sugar. Return to the boil then remove from the heat and allow to cool completely. Pour over the turkey, so it is fully immersed, cover and refrigerate for 3 to 6 hours.

To make the herb crust, put the sage and parsley, olive oil, lemon juice and pine nuts in a food processor and whiz for about 10 seconds, until you have a bright green oil. Put the mixture in a bowl and stir through the parmesan.

Remove the turkey from the brine, discarding the liquid. Pat dry with paper towel and put into a flat non-metallic dish. Rub the sauce all over the turkey, cover with plastic wrap and set aside for 20 minutes.

Preheat the barbecue hotplate to low. Put the turkey on the hotplate, skin side down. You want to hear just a gentle sizzle when you do this. If it sizzles like crazy then the hotplate is too hot and the crust will burn.

Put the lid on the barbecue and cook the turkey for 10 minutes. Do not move the turkey as you want an even, golden crust to form on the skin side. Using a flat metal spatula, gently press down on the turkey occasionally. Turn the turkey over and cook for a further 15 minutes, with the lid on, leaving the heat on low so the turkey remains cooking with a gentle sizzling sound, pressing down occasionally. Remove the turkey, wrap in foil and sit on the warm barbecue lid for 10 minutes. Remove the turkey to a plate and leave to stand for another 15 minutes before cutting into slices to serve.

1 whole turkey breast fillet (about 800 g/1 lb 12 oz), with skin on
130 g (4¾ oz/½ cup) table salt
75 g (2½ oz/⅓ cup) sugar

Herb crust
10–12 sage leaves
1 small bunch flat-leaf (Italian) parsley, leaves only, chopped
80 ml (2½ fl oz/⅓ cup) olive oil
3 tablespoons lemon juice
80 g (2¾ oz/½ cup) pine nuts
50 g (1¾ oz) parmesan cheese, finely grated

BEAST ESSENTIALS

Barbecued food is like nothing else and it is the beast that comes into its own when barbecued. There are other beasts, of course, but I have kept the recipes here for those easy-to-get—beef, pork and lamb—popular creatures, and despite being Australian I've never sat down to a plate of barbecued kangaroo or emu. It's rump steak for me. Marinated with a few Asian staples, cooked quickly. Say no more.

Spoilt for choice, we Antipodeans can hardly be blamed for our fondness of lamb in all its glory—neat little steaks, trimmed cutlets and meaty chops with just a decadent layer of fat. Let's not forget the special rack, no longer trussed up like a wallflower but flavoured and cooked to be eaten.

This is the chapter for crisp-skinned pork flavoured with addictive, smoky paprika, unctuous beef ribs given some voodoo magic with creole spice, Penang satay skewers, T-bone Florentine, Berber lamb and the glorious glazed Christmas ham, for the traditionalists out there. Take the kitchen outside.

Barbecued beast is only limited by your imagination. Marinating, resting and cooking time is the key to cooking these creatures. The beast is not a delicate creature, lamb excepted, so strong-flavoured bastes, spice rubs and sauces can be used. Explore longer marinating times and always bring the meat out of the fridge for a short time so it comes to room temperature before cooking. Red meat does not have the nasty bugs like those in chicken.

After cooking always allow the meat to rest. Heating the meat tightens the fibres, making hot meat tough. So let it relax and chill out a bit, covered with cooking foil. If you haven't been doing this already you will wonder what you have been missing all this time.

PENANG BEEF SATAY

SERVES 4 AS A SNACKY STARTER

Penang satay marinade
4 spring onions (scallions),
white part only, chopped
80 g (2¾ oz/½ cup)
crushed peanuts
2 tablespoons good-quality
curry powder
125 ml (4 fl oz/½ cup)
condensed milk
125 ml (4 fl oz/½ cup)
coconut cream
2 tablespoons fish sauce
½ teaspoon turmeric
2 tablespoons brown sugar

400 g (14 oz) beef
rump steak

Some recipes stand out. For me they can do this in two ways. Some recipes, when you read them, sound a bit odd and others, when you make them, really taste good. This is both. I first made this some time ago while researching traditional southern Thai and northern Malay satay sauces. Several recipes had condensed milk listed in the ingredients. My initial reaction was very much 'what the ...?' until I made this. The sweetness of the milk caramelises making this a rich affair so I think it really needs the home-made chilli sauce, spiked with lots of vinegar, drizzled over. Possibly, maybe, the best beef satay ever.

Put all the ingredients for the satay marinade in a food processor and whiz until you have a quite runny, yellow-curry-coloured marinade. Pour into a non-metallic dish.

Put the beef on a chopping board and slice on an angle going across the grain into thin 10–12 cm (4–4½ in) strips. Put the beef into the satay marinade, separate the pieces and massage the marinade into the meat. Cover and refrigerate for 3 to 6 hours or overnight if you have the time.

Remove the beef from the fridge 1 hour before cooking and soak sixteen wooden skewers. Thread 2 to 3 pieces of meat onto each skewer, reserving the marinade.

Preheat the barbecue hotplate to high and drizzle with a little olive oil to grease. Put the satay sticks on the hotplate and cook for 4 minutes, brushing a little remaining marinade onto the beef. The cooked side should develop a dark golden crust. Turn over and cook for another 3 to 4 minutes. Remove to a platter and serve with home-made sweet chilli sauce (page 212) for a delicious combination of flavours.

SPARE RIBS WITH BLACK PEPPER AND HONEY

SERVES 4

1 kg (2 lb 4 oz) pork spare ribs (American-style ribs)
2 tablespoons vegetable oil
1 tablespoon finely grated ginger
3 garlic cloves, finely chopped
3 shallots, finely chopped
1 tablespoon freshly ground black pepper
250 ml (9 fl oz/1 cup) chicken stock
175 g (6 oz/½ cup) honey

If you like Chinese food you will love these. I frequent a little hole-in-the-wall Chinese restaurant that serves up a dish that was the inspiration for this. It is no doubt all done in a wok in the restaurant but adapted here for the barbecue. You may have a barbecue with a wok gas hob but if you don't, fear not. The trick here is to cook them in a roasting tray sitting directly on the hotplate.

Cut between each rib. Arrange the ribs in a bamboo steamer lined with baking paper. Cover the steamer and sit on a large saucepan or wok of boiling water and cook for 30 minutes.

Meanwhile, heat 1 tablespoon of the oil in a saucepan on high heat and cook the ginger, garlic and shallots for 2 minutes, until aromatic and softened. Add the pepper, stock and honey and bring to the boil for 5 minutes, until slightly thickened.

Preheat the barbecue hotplate to high and sit a roasting tray on the hotplate. Add the remaining oil to the tray and cook the ribs for 10 minutes, turning them frequently so they cook to a golden brown all over. Add the sauce and bring to the boil. Cook for about 10 minutes, turning the ribs often, until the sauce is dark and thickly coats the ribs.

MINTY SALMORIGLIO LAMB STEAKS

Salmoriglio is a flavour-packed southern Italian herb concoction, usually made solely with oregano leaves, but here I've added some mint—making this sexy sauce a very suitable partner to some equally sexy little lamb rump steaks. Oh, and this is as quick as they come, in terms of preparation, marinating and cooking times.

Pound the oregano, mint, garlic and sea salt to a paste using a mortar and pestle or whiz in a small food processor. Stir through the oil and lemon juice and set aside for the flavours to develop.

Put the lamb steaks in a non-metallic dish and evenly coat with the sauce. Cover and set aside for 1 hour, or if it's a really hot day just leave it for 30 minutes. You can make this and place in the refrigerator a few hours in advance, but if you do so just add the lemon juice 30 minutes before cooking.

Preheat the barbecue grill to high and brush with a little light olive oil to grease. Put the lamb steaks on the grill and cook for 2 minutes on each side, with the lid on. Put on a plate, cover and rest for about 5 minutes. Serve with lemon wedges.

Next time: Lamb is not always an easy thing to find (outside the Antipodes, where people are spoilt for any cut of lamb) and it may be expensive where you are. But the lamb can be replaced with tuna steaks, or other full-flavoured, oily fish, and cooked accordingly.

handful oregano leaves
1 small bunch mint leaves
2 garlic cloves, chopped
1 teaspoon sea salt
2 tablespoons olive oil
1 tablespoon lemon juice
8 x 100 g (3½ oz) lamb rump steaks
lemon wedges, to serve

VEAL CUTLETS WITH ROSEMARY, ANCHOVY AND RED WINE

SERVES 4

The recipe is a cinch. The flavourings are classic and simple, paying respect to the lovely and very special (yes, I know, they are not the easiest things to find) veal cutlets.

Put the rosemary, anchovies and garlic in a mortar with a generous pinch of sea salt and some freshly ground black pepper. Pound until the anchovies are mashed. Put the mixture into a bowl and stir through the olive oil and red wine.

Put the cutlets in a non-metallic dish and pour over the marinade, tossing the cutlets around to coat in the mixture. Cover and refrigerate for 3 hours or overnight, turning them often.

Remove the cutlets from the fridge 1 hour before cooking.

Preheat the barbecue hotplate or grill to high. Put the cutlets on the hotplate or grill and cook for 5 minutes with the lid on the barbecue. They should look quite dark from the marinade. Turn over and cook for another 5 minutes, again with the lid on. Turn the barbecue heat off, lightly wrap the meat in cooking foil and sit on the warm lid for 5 minutes. Remove from the lid and rest for another 10 minutes in the foil before eating.

1 tablespoon rosemary leaves
3 anchovies
3 garlic cloves, chopped
3 tablespoons olive oil
125 ml (4 fl oz/½ cup) red wine
4 x veal cutlets, about 250 g (9 oz) each

HUNGARIAN PORK RACK

SERVES 4

Hungarian spice mix
1 teaspoon fennel seeds
1 teaspoon caraway seeds
1 teaspoon hot Hungarian
paprika
1 teaspoon sea salt
½ teaspoon freshly ground
black pepper

800 g–1 kg (1 lb 12 oz–
2 lb 4 oz) rack of pork, with
4 cutlets, skin scored

Do you find yourself getting occasional, obsessive crushes on an ingredient or flavour? For me, this time around it is the sexy, smoky Hungarian paprika. You may have to hunt a pack down at a European deli, but it does keep for ages, well sealed. This pork is a knockout and if you can, and I say this in full awareness of its scarcity, try cooking with free-range or organic pork. There really is nothing like it.

Pound all the spices together with a mortar and pestle, until the seeds are lightly crushed. Set aside.

Remove the pork from the fridge. Rub the spice mixture all over the skin and meat at either ends of the rack. Cover and set aside for 1 hour.

Preheat the barbecue hotplate to high and cover with the lid to create a hot-oven effect. Sit the pork on a rack and sit the rack over a deep baking tray. Half fill the baking tray with water and sit on the barbecue. Cover with the lid and cook for 30 minutes, until the skin is just starting to crisp up around the edges. Turn the heat down to low–medium and cook for 1½ hours. You may have to rotate the pork around on the rack as some sides may start to cook quicker than the others. The pork should start to look dark golden all over and the skin should start to crisp up around the edges. For really crunchy crackling, turn the heat to high, cover and cook for 5 to 10 minutes longer. Remove and lightly cover with foil for 30 minutes before carving.

T-BONE FLORENTINE

Despite its fancy-pants name this is the style of cooking that is the essence of a great barbecue—the meat is the star attraction with a couple of support acts on the side. Choose a great bit of meat, I use T-bone because it is one of the few cuts of beef with a bone that can be easily barbecued, except maybe for ribs but these aren't always available or affordable.

Remove your steaks from the fridge 45 minutes to 1 hour before barbecuing. This will allow the meat to come to room temperature. The cooking time is quite quick here and because the meat is on the bone the centres of the steak will be cold if cooked straight from the fridge. Rub the cut garlic halves all over the T-bones, including the bone.

Preheat the barbecue grill to high and brush with a little olive oil to grease.

Rub the cut lemons over the steaks and then cook the lemons on the grill for 5 minutes, until they are scored and starting to caramelise.

Remove and set aside. Rub the meat with about 1 tablespoon of olive oil and sprinkle the salt on both sides of the steaks. Put the steaks on the grill and cook for 4 minutes. Turn over and cook for another 4 minutes for medium-rare. Serve with the parsley sprinkled over and grilled lemons on the side to squeeze.

4 T-bone steaks, about 2 cm (¾ in) thick at the bone
2 garlic cloves, cut in half
4 lemons, cut in half
1 tablespoon sea salt
2 tablespoons roughly chopped flat-leaf (Italian) parsley, to serve

LAMB RACK WITH FETA AND PRESERVED LEMON

SERVES 4

2 racks of lamb (each with 8 cutlets), preferably organic, about 600 g (1 lb 5 oz) each
100 g (3½ oz/²/₃ cup) soft feta cheese (preferably a marinated feta, really soft in tasty oil)
1½ tablespoons chopped preserved lemon
12 large mint leaves, finely chopped

I like to use organic lamb racks. They generally have a nice layer of fat hugging one side and this is good to put flavourings on, under and around. You will need some type of cooking rack for this, a cake rack is fine or grab one of the racks from your oven. This recipe cooks a piece of lamb quite pink in the centre—just how lamb should be eaten, really.

Slice several incisions under the layer of fat where it meets the skin on the lamb racks.

Put the feta, lemon and mint in a small bowl with some freshly ground black pepper, mash with the back of a fork and add just a splash of the tasty oil from the marinated feta or some olive oil to combine. Use a teaspoon or your fingers to work this mixture into the incisions, forcing in as much as you can. Put into a non-metallic dish, cover and refrigerate for a day or two.

Remove the racks from the fridge 1 hour before cooking.

Preheat the barbecue hotplate to medium. Put 2 sheets of foil on a rack. Put the lamb racks on the hotplate, skin side down, cover with the lid and cook for 5 minutes, until golden. Turn over to cook for another 5 minutes, covering the barbecue with its lid. Now put the lamb on the cooking rack and sit the rack on the hotplate. Put the lid on and cook for 10 minutes. Remove the lamb to a plate, lightly cover with foil and rest for 10 minutes. Carve each rack in half to give four portions or cut between all the bones for sixteen individual cutlets.

SHEFTALIA

Sheftalia is a traditional Greek and Cypriot grilled meat recipe—lamb mince with a few other simple seasonings thrown in. It's lovely wrapped in warm pitta bread with a Mediterranean salad (page 205) and some extra feta dressing dolloped all over.

Put the lamb mince in a large bowl with the garlic, parsley, oregano, 1 teaspoon of sea salt and some freshly ground black pepper. Use your hands to combine the meat with the other flavourings, throwing the meat against the side of the bowl so the meat begins to look like a paste. Lightly wet your hands with water and divide the mixture into sixteen equal parts, then roll each into a ball, about the size of a golf ball. Put on a tray, cover and refrigerate for 3 hours or overnight.

Remove the meatballs from the fridge 30 minutes before cooking.

Preheat the barbecue hotplate to medium and drizzle with a little olive oil to grease. Put the meatballs on the grill and cook for 5 minutes, gently pressing down with a flat metal spatula so they look more like a disc or a small burger pattie. Turn over and cook for 5 minutes. Remove to a plate and top with the yoghurt and mint, and sprinkle the cayenne over. Serve in warm pita rolls with salad.

700 g (1 lb 9 oz) minced (ground) lamb
4 garlic cloves, crushed
2 tablespoons finely chopped flat-leaf (Italian) parsley
1 tablespoon finely chopped oregano
4 soft pitta breads, to serve
cayenne pepper, to serve

RUMP STEAK WITH GINGER, GARLIC AND SOY

SERVES 4

Ginger soy marinade
125 ml (4 fl oz/½ cup)
light soy sauce,
preferably Japanese
1 tablespoon sesame oil
½ teaspoon sugar
2 garlic cloves,
roughly chopped
5 cm (2 in) piece ginger,
peeled and very
finely sliced

2 x 400 g (14 oz) pieces
beef rump steak,
about 1.5 cm (⅝ in) thick

Here is my earliest barbecue memory—eating a steak, marinated in these Asian flavours, pool side at Aunty Betty's in the Sydney summer. You can't go past rump. I still like to throw it out there at barbecues and ask people what their favourite cut of barbecued steak is. Most say rump. If you are lucky enough to get a really big piece of rump you will see how it is divided into several muscle groups, which are separated by lines of fat.

Put the ginger soy marinade ingredients in a small bowl and stir to combine. Put the pieces of rump in a large non-metallic dish and pour over the marinade. Cover and set aside for 1 hour, turning the pieces often. You could put the steaks in the fridge for a couple of hours but be aware the salt in the soy can make the meat tough. I find the steak has a better flavour and texture if left to marinate at room temperature for a short time.

Preheat the barbecue grill to high and brush with a little vegetable oil to grease. Put the steaks on the grill and cook for 3 minutes on each side. Remove the steaks to a plate, cover lightly with foil and rest for 5 minutes. The steaks will be quite pink in the centre, medium-rare. If you'd prefer the steaks less pink, cook for 5 minutes each side for medium and 7 minutes each side for well done. Cut each steak in half to serve 4 or into several smaller pieces as part of a barbecue banquet.

HOT DOGS WITH BEER-BRAISED ONIONS

SERVES 4

I will admit, the idea of cooking a hot dog, or a hamburger for that matter, on the barbecue is very American. The frankfurters are of course already cooked, you are just heating them through. So do try and get your hands on some good veal frankfurters from a European deli. The recipe here is really all about the onions which can be used on many other barbecue occasions.

4 veal frankfurters
3 large white onions
125 ml (4 fl oz/½ cup) beer
1 tablespoon butter
4 hot dog buns, to serve
German mustard, to serve

Preheat the barbecue burners to high and brush the hotplate and grill with a little vegetable oil to grease.

Prick your frankfurters all over with a fork. Put the frankfurters on the grill and the onions on the hotplate. Push the pile of onions around with your barbecue tongs to spread them out in a single layer. Keep turning your frankfurters every 2 minutes, until they are starting to just get little char marks, and keep tossing the onions on the hotplate. Now put the frankfurters in among the onions and pour a couple of tablespoons of beer over the frankfurters and onions causing the hotplate to sizzle. When the beer has evaporated keep adding a little more at a time to the hotplate until all the beer has been used up. When the onions are golden add the butter and cook for a few more minutes until the onions turn an amber ale colour.

To serve, butter the hot dog buns and spread with the mustard. Add the frankfurters and onions.

CAB SAV BEEF RIBS

SERVES 4

2 x 1 kg (2 lb 4 oz) or
4 x 350–400 g (12–14 oz)
grain-fed beef rib eye
on the bone
500 ml (17 fl oz/2 cups) good
quality cabernet sauvignon
1 garlic bulb, cloves
separated and left unpeeled,
lightly crushed
4 sprigs dried oregano

This recipe was originally written and made using four beef rib eyes, each about 350–400 g. In chatting with a butcher, I was lured into getting two huge single rib eyes, each weighing almost 1 kg (2 lb 4 oz). Check one of these out in all its glory as it sits on page 91, a beautifully marbled specimen. So don't be too freaked out when you read that the recipe calls for a piece like this, but the smaller ones will work a treat too. This is simple, best enjoyed with hotplate wedges and some of the cheat's béarnaise on page 206 as well.

Put the rib eyes in a large non-metallic dish and pour over the red wine. Add the other ingredients with ½ teaspoon of freshly ground black pepper and toss the ribs around making sure they don't overlap too much. Cover and refrigerate overnight, turning often.

Remove the rib eyes from the fridge at least 1 hour before cooking so the marinade comes to room temperature.

Preheat the barbecue hotplate to high, drizzle with a little olive oil to grease, remove the ribs from the marinade and also brush a little oil on the rib eyes. Season with sea salt and cook the rib eyes for 5 minutes. Turn over and cook for another 5 minutes. Turn once more and cook for 1 minute. Wrap each of the rib eyes in foil and set aside to rest for 20 minutes. Serve with easy béarnaise sauce and hotplate wedges (page 213).

BERBER LAMB

Morocco is a crazy and exciting place and one recent visit there acted as an inspiration for barbecued food. Street-side stalls fire up and barbecue all sorts of meaty treats, day and night, and lamb and beef prevail. The flavours are addictive—lots of full-on spices combined with fresh herbs—and, here, the lamb is finished with sweet honey.

To make the Berber butter, reserve some of the fresh herbs and put the remaining herbs and all the other rub ingredients in a food processor. Whiz until finely chopped and very well combined, scraping down the sides of the bowl several times. Rub the herb and spice mix all over both sides of the lamb, cover and refrigerate overnight, turning often.

Remove the lamb from the fridge 1 hour before cooking.

Preheat all the barbecue burners to medium and put the lid on. Cover a cooking rack with two layers of foil. Sit the rack on a baking tin half-filled with water. Sit the lamb on the rack and put the tin on the barbecue hotplate. Cover and cook for 20 minutes until the skin starts to sizzle. Reduce all the burners to low. Loosely cover the lamb with foil, so it doesn't burn, and cook for 1½ hours. Remove the lamb to a serving plate, cover with foil and allow the lamb to rest for 30 minutes. Drizzle over the honey and reserved herbs to serve.

Berber butter rub
1 small bunch coriander (cilantro), chopped
1 small bunch flat-leaf (Italian) parsley, chopped
4 garlic cloves, chopped
1 tablespoon chopped ginger
1 red chilli, seeded and chopped
1 small bunch mint, roughly chopped
1 tablespoon ground coriander
1 tablespoon ground cumin
2 tablespoons butter
1 tablespoon olive oil

1 small leg of lamb, about 2–2.25 kg (4 lb 8 oz–5 lb), butterflied
115 g (4 oz/⅓ cup) honey, at room temperature

CHRISTMAS BARBECUED GLAZED HAM

SERVES MANY

2 x 450 g (1 lb) tins
pineapple rings
45 g (1¾ oz/¼ cup)
light brown sugar
2 tablespoons mild mustard
2 x 100 g (3½ oz) packets
glace cherries
1 whole cooked leg ham,
about 8–9 kg (17–19 lb)
2 tablespoons whole cloves

In my book a garnish is something that should be eaten, except for any ingredients you use on a Christmas ham to make it look pretty. The glazed ham is a beautiful thing, but it is all smoke and mirrors really to get it to look good. The ham is already cooked, of course, so all you are doing is making it look drop-dead gorgeous; the star of the Christmas lunch table and the good thing is all this can be done to equal effect on the barbie, leaving your oven and kitchen free for all the other Christmas day fussing.

Drain the pineapple and measure the liquid. You will need 500 ml (17 fl oz/2 cups) of liquid. If you don't have enough pineapple juice, make up the rest with water or orange juice. Slice each pineapple ring through the centre to give two thinner rings. Put the juice in a frying pan with the sugar and mustard and cook over medium heat, stirring until the sugar dissolves. Boil for 5 minutes so the liquid thickens a little. Add the rings and toss them to coat in the juice, then cook for 5 minutes so the rings darken just a little. Set aside to cool.

Preheat all the barbecue burners to medium, with the lid on to create an oven-type effect.

To remove the skin from the ham, cut a line through the thick rind a few centimetres from the shank end with a sharp knife. Run your thumb around the edge and carefully pull back the skin, leaving the fat on the leg. When the skin is removed, lightly score the fat in a diamond pattern (if you score too deeply the fat will fall off during the cooking process).

Start to arrange the pineapple rings on the fat, starting at the shank end. Secure the rings with one or two cloves then secure a glace cherry in the centre of each ring with a clove. Repeat so the ham is covered all over with the pineapple and cherries.

Half fill a large roasting tray with water. Sit the ham on a cooking rack and sit this on top of the tray. Brush some of the pineapple glaze over the ham and put on the barbecue. Cover with the lid. Now you simply have to cook the ham until it looks good. This will take about 1½ to 2 hours, brushing more glaze over the ham every 20 minutes or so and making sure the water doesn't dry out, until the pineapple rings are almost dark caramel in colour and some of the fat and juices of the ham have dripped down forming toffee stalactites around the sides.

Allow to rest for 30 minutes before carving.

JERK LAMB CHOPS

SERVES 4

Jerk paste
2 teaspoons allspice
⅛ teaspoon fresh
grated nutmeg
1 teaspoon ground ginger
1 teaspoon freshly ground
black pepper
2 teaspoons dried thyme
1 teaspoon dried marjoram
2 tablespoons light
brown sugar
2 tablespoon light soy sauce

4 x lamb fore-quarter chops,
not very thick, about
1 cm (½ in)
1 lime, cut in half

This intensely flavoured rub is traditionally used on strong-flavoured meats like goat and mutton but for our purposes here we have used lamb chops—much more barbecue friendly.

First, make your jerk paste blend. Combine all the ingredients in a bowl and stir until you have a thick, dark and very aromatic paste. Set aside for the flavours to develop. (This can even be made a few hours or a day in advance.)

Put the lamb chops in a snug-fitting non-metallic dish, pour over the paste and rub the spice mixture all over the lamb. Cover and refrigerate overnight so the flavours really penetrate the meat, or you could leave to sit at room temperature for 2 to 3 hours.

Remove the chops from the fridge 30 minutes before cooking.

Preheat the barbecue grill to high and brush with a little vegetable oil to grease. Put the lamb on the grill and cook for 3 minutes on each side, so they are just starting to char around the edges and the jerk paste has cooked to a dark colour all over the lamb. Remove, cover with cooking foil for 5 minutes to rest before serving.

FAJITA RUMP STEAK
WITH MASHED AVOCADO

There is a story here. Apparently the word 'faja' is Spanish for belt or girdle. Traditionally, a fajita would really use skirt steak, a cut of meat popular in North America. I have tried this both with skirt and rump and I am unconvinced about all the fuss made about this skirt steak—it is an overly tough piece of meat. The steak here, rump of course, could be served with just about any of the sides—especially hotplate wedges (page 213), coleslaw (page 211) or herb-marinated potato salad (page 210).

Put the marinade ingredients in a non-metallic dish and stir around well so you have the sort of marinade that looks like something you would dip a corn chip into. Add the steaks and toss them around to really coat in the marinade. Cover the bowl and refrigerate for 3 to 6 hours.

Remove the steaks from the fridge 1 hour before cooking.

Preheat the barbecue hotplate to high and drizzle with a little olive oil to grease. Shake the excess marinade off the steaks, put on the hotplate and cook for 3 minutes on each side. You want the steaks to really sizzle for their short cooking time. Remove the steak on to a plate, lightly cover in foil, and leave to rest for 5 minutes.

Put the flesh of the avocado in a bowl with the salt and mash well. Add a squeeze of lime juice if you like and serve with the fajita steak wrapped in a warm burrito.

Fajita marinade
1 small bunch coriander (cilantro), leaves only, finely chopped
2 tablespoons lime juice
1 teaspoon chilli powder
1 tablespoon ground cumin
1 teaspoon Tabasco sauce
2 teaspoons olive oil

4 x beef rump steaks, about 200 g (7 oz) each
2 ripe avocados
1 teaspoon sea salt

VEAL CUTLETS WITH HERBS AND PROSCIUTTO

SERVES 4

The inspiration for this is the classic veal saltimbocca (jump in the mouth!). It's that quick-cook veal schnitzel cooked with one sage leaf, and a few extra bits. I always like the idea of this but it often leaves me a bit unsatisfied asking 'Why only one sage leaf?' True, sage is a strong herb, but it does seem all a bit twee to have but one. Here is a robust barbecue veal saltimbocca.

4 veal cutlets, about 250 g (9 oz) each
1 bunch sage
1 small bunch rosemary
1 small bunch thyme
8 thin slices prosciutto

Gently pound the veal cutlets to tenderise them. Grab a couple of sage leaves, with stems intact, a sprig of rosemary and a small sprig or two of thyme and place these on one side of the cutlet to form a little herbaceous clump. Grind some freshly ground black pepper over the top. Now take a piece of prosciutto and wrap around the veal. One piece may not be long enough to go entirely around the veal so use another piece to wrap around from where the two ends of the first piece don't meet up.

Preheat the barbecue hotplate to high and drizzle with a little olive oil to grease. Put the veal on the hotplate, herby-clump side down, and cook for 5 minutes, until the prosciutto looks crispy and the herbs cook and release oils to flavour the veal. Turn over and cook for another 5 minutes. Turn the barbecue off, wrap the veal in foil and sit on the hot barbecue lid for 10 minutes. Remove and allow to rest for another 5 minutes before serving.

PEPPER BEEF FILLET

SERVES 4

2 x 400 g (14 oz) best beef fillets (both from the mid cut so they are even sizes)
1 tablespoon white peppercorns
1 tablespoon black peppercorns
1 tablespoon olive oil
1 garlic bulb, cloves separated and lightly smashed
1 bunch thyme

A special piece of meat is this fillet—larger at one end and tapers down to a tail. Ask your butcher to give you two fillets which are even in size, to keep the cooking time the same. The tip here of shaking away the fine pepper powder is a good one. It ensures you get an intense pepper flavour without the unpalatable heat. But a couple of things to remember when using this prime cut—make use of the hot lid of the barbecue in finishing off the cooking and do remember to let the meat rest.

Trim the meat of any excess fat and put in a non-metallic dish.

Put all the peppercorns in a spice mill and roughly grind. Put the pepper in a sieve and shake away the fine powder. Rub the remaining rough powder all over the beef fillets. Put in the refrigerator and leave uncovered overnight, turning a few times. You can do this up to 2 days in advance.

Remove the beef from the fridge and add the olive oil, garlic and thyme to the dish, turning the beef. Set aside for 1 hour.

Preheat the barbecue hotplate to medium. Put the beef fillets on the hotplate and cook for 8 minutes with the lid on, turning every 2 minutes, so that each surface (including the sides) is cooked for the same length of time. Turn the barbecue off and wrap the meat in two layers of foil. Sit the beef on top of the warm lid of the barbecue for 10 minutes. Remove to a plate and leave to rest, still wrapped in the foil, for 10 minutes.

Cut the beef into thick slices and serve with easy béarnaise sauce (page 206) if you like.

CHINATOWN PORK

You see these unctuous and shiny glazed morsels hanging in Chinatown windows. It's probably a toss-up between the roast duck and the barbecue pork (or char siu) as to which is the most popular. The roast duck is one of those things you would never really want to cook at home. The pork on the other hand is dead easy. All you need are a few Chinatown grocery staples (sauces that will keep for ages in the cupboard) and away you go.

Put all the glaze ingredients in a non-metallic dish and stir around until combined. Add the pork fillets and rub the glaze all over the pork. Cover and refrigerate for 3 hours. Don't marinate it for any longer—the salt content is quite high and, left too long, the meat will become tough and chewy.

Remove the pork from the fridge 30 minutes before cooking.

Preheat the barbecue hotplate to medium. Sit the pork on a cooking rack and sit the rack on a roasting tin half-filled with water. Cook for 20 minutes, turning and basting with the marinade every 2 to 3 minutes. The fillet will have shrunk a little and should look beautiful reddish-brown and be charred in some places. Remove and allow to cool to room temperature before cutting each fillet in half or finely slicing onto a serving plate.

Char siu glaze
1 teaspoon Chinese
five-spice powder
2 tablespoons honey
2 tablespoons hoi sin sauce
2 tablespoons light soy sauce

2 pork fillets, about 400 g
(14 oz) each

TANDOORI RACK OF LAMB

SERVES 4

Tandoori paste
1 small red onion
2 garlic cloves
2 teaspoons finely
grated ginger
150 g (5½ oz/½ cup) good-
quality shop-bought
tandoori paste
125 g (4½ oz/½ cup)
natural yoghurt
½ teaspoon smoked paprika

4 racks of lamb,
each with 4 cutlets

This Indian adaptation is full of short cuts. Instead of making my own tandoori paste recipe I'm cheating here, using a shop-bought one (and there are heaps of good brands on the market). I do whiz in a couple of fresh ingredients though to make me feel like I have contributed to this dead-simple recipe.

Put the onion, garlic and ginger in a food processor and whiz so they are finely chopped. Add the tandoori paste, yoghurt and paprika and whiz again until well combined and you have a light-orange thick paste.

Put the lamb racks in a non-metallic dish and rub the paste all over, avoiding the bones. Sit the lamb in the dish so the bones point upward, cover and refrigerate overnight.

Preheat the barbecue hotplate to medium. Lightly drizzle the hotplate with a little vegetable oil to grease. Put the lamb racks on the hotplate and cook for 5 minutes, skin or fat side down, so the paste looks very well cooked, almost charred around the edges of the rack. Turn over and cook the racks for another 5 minutes. Wrap each rack in some foil, making sure the edges of the foil are firmly sealed and sit the wrapped lamb on a cooking rack. Sit the cooking rack on the hotplate, close the lid and cook for 15 minutes. Remove the lamb to a plate, leaving them wrapped in the foil to rest for 15 minutes. Serve a whole rack per person or carve into individual cutlets. The cooking time is for the lamb to be quite pink in the centre. For a medium lamb cook for an extra 2 minutes on each side when wrapped in the foil.

SPICY BEEF KEBABS

Don't you find that many skewered meats (kebabs) are tough? And try not to be tempted by those premade ones you see at the butchers. Here, the acid in the grated onion tenderises the meat in this Moroccan inspired recipe. And remember to leave the meat to rest at room temperature for a short while, both before and after cooking. The cooking time here is short and if cooked directly from the refrigerator the beef will be stone cold in the centre.

1 small onion
2 garlic cloves, crushed
2 teaspoons ground cumin
1 teaspoon paprika
1 teaspoon dried chilli flakes
1 handful coriander
(cilantro) leaves and stems
1 handful flat-leaf (Italian)
parsley leaves and stems
2 tablespoons lemon juice
600 g (1 lb 5 oz) thick cut
beef rump steak,
cut into chunky 2–3 cm
(¾–1¼ in) cubes
fresh lemon, to serve

Finely grate the onion so you have 2 tablespoons. Put the onion pulp into a small bowl with the garlic, cumin, paprika, chilli flakes, coriander parsley and lemon juice, and stir to combine. Soak some bamboo skewers.

Put the steak cubes in a non-metallic dish and add the spicy onion mix. Stir well so the meat is evenly covered in the spices or cover firmly with plastic food wrap and shake the bowl to combine the ingredients. Refrigerate for 3 to 6 hours, shaking the bowl from time to time.

Thread 3 to 4 pieces of meat onto a wooden skewer. Season each skewer well with sea salt and freshly ground black pepper. Set aside for 30 minutes.

Preheat the barbecue hotplate to high and drizzle with just enough olive oil to grease. Put the kebabs on the hotplate and cook for 8 minutes, turning every 2 minutes, until all the sides of the beef are brown. Remove to a serving plate and cover with foil to rest for 5 minutes. Squeeze over fresh lemon to serve.

PORK SHOULDER WITH FENNEL AND GARLIC

SERVES 6-8

2 tablespoons fennel seeds
6 garlic cloves, crushed
1 tablespoon sea salt
2 tablespoons white vinegar
1.5 kg (3 lb 5 oz) rolled
pork shoulder,
skin on
6 bay leaves
1 large fennel bulb,
thickly sliced

This as an autumnal barbecued favourite but need not be saved for the cooler months. One of the great benefits of barbecuing is you can cook these big cuts of meat outdoors in summer—getting out of that hot kitchen.

Pound the fennel seeds in a mortar and pestle until just split—don't pound them too finely. Add the garlic, salt and vinegar, and pound until they combine into a thick paste. Set aside.

Remove the pork from the fridge and use a sharp knife (a Stanley knife is ideal) to cut 5 mm (¼ in) deep incisions across the skin, about 1 to 2 cm (½ to ¾ in) apart. Smear the paste mixture over the meaty ends of the rolled pork and the skin, rubbing it into the cuts. Leave the pork to sit for 1 hour.

Preheat the barbecue hotplate and grill burners to high and close the lid to create a hot-oven effect. Put the bay leaves in a deep-sided baking tin. Pour enough boiling water in to come halfway up the sides. Put two layers of foil on a cooking rack and arrange the fennel slices in the centre. Sit the pork on the fennel, skin side up and cook for 45 minutes with the lid on until the fennel is tender and golden. Remove the fennel to a plate and cover. Turn all the burners down to low. Rotate the baking tin 180 degrees to promote even cooking and cook the pork for another 45 minutes to 1 hour, until the skin is crackling and dark golden. Remove to a serving plate, cover with foil and allow to rest for 20 minutes before carving. Serve with the fennel.

FILLET STEAK
WITH CAFE DE PARIS BUTTER

SERVES 4

This is amusing as it inspires much who-made-what-and-where debate. The original recipe is guarded as secretly as one Colonel Sanders' eleven secret herbs and spices. Some recipes list as many as thirty ingredients. But let's not get carried away. This is a barbecue after all. This version of Café de Paris butter only has ten ingredients but it is pretty bloody good. (PS: this will keep for ages in the fridge.)

To make the Café de Paris butter, put all the ingredients, except the butter, in a food processor and whiz until you have a chunky paste. Remove to a bowl, cover and leave at room temperature for a few hours for the flavours to develop.

Put the butter in a bowl and add the mixture. Stir for a few minutes, making sure the butter is evenly combined. Lay a sheet of plastic food wrap on a bench. Put spoonfuls of the butter along the centre of the plastic, then firmly wrap and form into a log. Refrigerate until needed. Remove the butter from the fridge to come to room temperature before using.

Put the beef fillets in a snug-fitting non-metallic dish. Add the red wine and olive oil, tossing the meat around to coat in the marinade. Cover and refrigerate overnight.

Remove the meat from the fridge 1 hour before cooking.

Preheat the barbecue grill to high and brush with a little olive oil to grease. Put the steak on the grill and cook for 5 minutes on each side. Wrap the meat in some foil and, leaving the heat on, close the lid and sit the meat on top for 5 minutes. Remove and allow to rest for another 10 minutes in the foil before serving with the butter sliced or spooned over the meat.

Café de Paris butter
1 tablespoon mild mustard
2 teaspoons worcestershire sauce
2 tablespoons tomato sauce (ketchup)
1 garlic clove
1 tablespoon capers, rinsed and well drained
6 anchovies
2 tablespoons roughly chopped flat-leaf (Italian) parsley
2 teaspoons thyme leaves
1 teaspoon Madras curry powder
250 g (9 oz) butter, softened

4 x 200 g (7 oz) thick-cut beef fillet steaks
250 ml (9 fl oz/1 cup) red wine
2 tablespoons olive oil

MUSTARD AND CORIANDER LAMB STEAKS

SERVES 6-8

1 small leg of lamb,
about 1.8 kg (4 lb)
3 tablespoons olive oil
3 tablespoons lemon juice
1 garlic bulb, cloves
separated and left unpeeled,
lightly crushed
2 tablespoons Dijon mustard
2 teaspoons ground
coriander
1 teaspoon freshly ground
black pepper
1 bunch fresh coriander
(cilantro), finely chopped

The idea here is to cut off thick steaks from the leg to look like porterhouse or New York cuts. At a pinch you could try getting away with marinating this for a few hours but it is far superior in flavour if left overnight.

Trim the lamb of any excess fat then cut the leg into thick steaks, across the leg, a bit like porterhouse steaks, about 3 to 4 cm (1¼ to 1½ in) wide and 2 to 3 cm (¾ to 1¼ in) thick. Put the lamb into a non-metallic dish, mix together the other ingredients and rub all over the lamb. Cover and refrigerate overnight, turning often.

Remove the lamb from the fridge 1 hour before cooking.

Preheat the barbecue hotplate to high. Put the lamb on the hotplate and cook for 4 minutes on each side with the lid on, brushing with some of the marinade. Some of the pieces will have irregular shapes, especially those from the thicker part of the leg. Cook any uncooked sides on these larger pieces for an extra 2 minutes. Leave the barbecue on and wrap the lamb pieces in foil. Close the lid and sit the meat on the top for 5 minutes. Remove to a plate and leave in the foil to rest for another 15 minutes. Serve the pieces of meat whole or carve into strips.

CHEESEBURGERS

Use these tasty mince patties between a couple of buns with tomato, onions, lettuce and beetroot for the ultimate Aussie hamburger experience (sorry, I draw the line at pineapple). The kids will love these cooked on the barbecue and finished off with a slice of tasty cheddar melted on top. And they'll be great for the adults too!

1 tablespoon olive oil
1 small onion, finely chopped
1 bacon slice, finely chopped
1 garlic clove, crushed
1 teaspoon dried mixed herbs
500 g (1 lb 2 oz) minced (ground) beef
1 egg
4 slices cheddar cheese

Heat the oil in a small frying pan over medium heat and cook the onion and bacon for about 2 to 3 minutes until the onions are soft. Add the garlic and dried herbs, cook for another minute then remove from the heat. Put in a bowl and allow to cool to room temperature. Add the beef and egg, and season well with sea salt and freshly ground black pepper. Use your hands to really combine all the ingredients. Divide into four and firmly roll each into a ball. Flatten each ball into a burger-like pattie and put on a plate lined with baking paper, cover and refrigerate until needed. These can be made the day before.

Remove the patties from the fridge 30 minutes before cooking.

Preheat the barbecue hotplate to medium and drizzle with a little olive oil to grease. Put the patties on the hotplate and cook for 6 minutes, letting them gently sizzle. Turn over and cook for another 5 minutes, until they are evenly brown all over. Cook for another 2 minutes on each side for a well-done pattie. Put a slice of cheese on each pattie, close the lid and cook for another 2 minutes, until the cheese has melted.

Put the patties on buns and top with a combination of fillings and sauces.

TOPSIDE STEAK SANDWICHES WITH BALSAMIC ONIONS AND GARLIC CREME

serves 4

Garlic crème
10–12 garlic cloves, peeled
1 tablespoon sweet
German mustard
2 egg yolks
125 ml (4 fl oz/
½ cup) olive oil

Balsamic onions
6 red onions
2 tablespoons olive oil
1 tablespoon
balsamic vinegar
handful flat-leaf (Italian)
parsley, roughly chopped

600 g (1 lb 5 oz)
topside steak
3 tablespoons olive oil
6 rosemary sprigs
4 soft bread rolls
3 tomatoes, thinly sliced
2 large handfuls baby rocket
(arugula)

You can use a whole piece of topside for this and slice it yourself. Look for a piece of meat that is nicely (and by this I mean substantially) marbled throughout the whole cut.

To make the garlic crème, preheat the barbecue hotplate to medium. Tear off a sheet of cooking foil, put the garlic in the centre and loosely wrap. Sit the foil-wrapped garlic on the hotplate and cook for 20 minutes, it should be able to squash a little when squeezed. Put the cooked garlic directly into a food processor. Add the mustard, egg yolks and season well with sea salt and freshly ground black pepper. Process for a few seconds to combine and with the motor running gradually pour in the oil until you have a thick custard-like mixture. Put in a bowl, cover and refrigerate until needed.

Trim any excess fat from the topside, but leave a little on the edge and cut into eight thin slices. Put a piece of meat between two layers of plastic food wrap and gently pound so it is an even thickness all over, less than 5 mm (¼ in) thick, then cut in half. Put in a non-metallic dish with the olive oil, rosemary, garlic and pepper, then set aside for 30 minutes.

Meanwhile, peel the onions and cut into 5 mm (¼ in) wide rounds. With the hotplate on medium, drizzle a little olive oil over and spread evenly with a flat metal spatula. Put the onions on the hotplate and leave them to sizzle gently for 8 to 10 minutes. Like many successful barbecue recipes, the trick here is a simple one—be patient! Don't turn the onions over until thye are really dark golden, which indicates they have caramelised and are turning that lovely sweet and charred barbecued flavour we know and love. Turn them over and let them do the same thing on the other side for 8 to 10 minutes. Put the onions in a heatproof bowl with the remaining oil, vinegar, parsley and a good seasoning of sea salt and freshly ground black pepper. Move to a warm place on the barbecue, away from direct heat and leave for at least 30 minutes for the flavours to really develop.

Preheat the barbecue grill to high. Season the meat well with sea salt. Put the steak on the grill and cook for 2 minutes on each side until evenly browned. Remove to a plate.

Lightly butter the rolls then spread a little of the garlic crème on each side. Put 2 to 3 pieces of meat on the bottom half, top with a spoonful of balsamic onions, tomatoes and rocket, then serve.

STEAK WITH MUSHROOMS

SERVES 4

4 thick beef rump steaks,
about 180 g (6½ oz) each
125 ml (4 fl oz/½ cup)
light soy sauce
2 tablespoons
balsamic vinegar
1 tablespoon grated ginger
3 garlic cloves,
roughly chopped
16 shiitake mushrooms,
stems removed
2 tablespoons butter,
roughly chopped

I don't know why, but I think of this as a summer night dinner recipe. The mushrooms marinate with the meat and are quickly cooked on the hotplate until they just start to caramelise. Perfect with a good red.

Put the steaks in a non-metallic dish with the soy, vinegar, ginger and garlic. Add the mushrooms and toss around so the mushrooms and the steaks are covered in the marinade. Cover and refrigerate for 3 hours.

Remove the steak and mushrooms from the fridge 30 minutes before cooking.

Preheat the barbecue hotplate to high and drizzle with a little olive oil to grease. Cook the steaks for 4 minutes on each side for medium-rare. Remove to a plate and cover with foil to rest.

Put the mushrooms on the hotplate, top side down, and pour the marinade into the caps of the mushrooms. Cover the barbecue with a lid and cook for 3 to 4 minutes. Turn over and cook for 2 minutes. The caps should be dark golden and the mushrooms very soft. Put the butter pieces over the mushrooms and cook for 1 minute, until the butter has just melted and quickly spoon the mushrooms over the steaks.

FRUITY LAMB FILLETS

Tomato chutney is an institution, and any commercial, sweet tomato-based fruit chutney will do. Again this is sensible fusion with a few tricks making for an easy barbecue recipe you will want to repeat.

Put the lamb fillets in a snug-fitting non-metallic dish. Combine the remaining ingredients in a small bowl, pour over the lamb and rub all over the lamb. Cover and refrigerate overnight, turning the meat from time to time.

Remove the meat from the fridge 1 hour before cooking.

Preheat the barbecue grill to high and brush with some olive oil to grease. Season the lamb fillets with sea salt and freshly ground black pepper, put on the grill and cook for 3 minutes on each side with the lid on. Wrap the lamb in foil, turn the barbecue off and sit the meat on the hot lid for 5 minutes. Remove and allow the meat to rest for another 10 minutes in the foil before unwrapping and slicing thickly across the grain to serve.

2 large lamb backstrap fillets, about 350–400 g (12–14 oz) each
140 g (5 oz/½ cup) tomato and fruit chutney
1 teaspoon ground cumin
1 teaspoon ground coriander
2 tablespoons Chinese rice wine
2 tablespoons lemon juice

HAVANA SPICED PORK CHOPS WITH ORANGE SHERRY ONIONS

I have never been to Cuba and it has become a bit of a fantasy of mine to go there. Cuban food is a hodgepodge of tropical, European and Creole elements, a laid-back peasant-based cuisine unconcerned with getting bogged down in measurements. You will often see lime juice or sour orange juice used in a marinade, especially with pork. It's all pretty chilled out, like their music.

Put the pork chops in a snug-fitting non-metallic dish and pour over the rum, juices and garlic. Cover and refrigerate overnight, turning often.

Remove the pork chops from the marinade 30 minutes before cooking, pat dry with paper towel and rest on a tray lined with baking paper. Add the onions to the marinade, tossing them around to separate the rings and set aside.

Combine the oregano, cumin and cayenne pepper in a small bowl and sprinkle the dry spice mix on both sides of the chops.

Preheat the barbecue hotplate to medium and drizzle with a little vegetable oil to lightly grease. Put the chops on the hotplate and cook for 7 minutes, until they are a rich golden colour. Turn over and cook for another 5 minutes. Remove to a serving plate, cover with foil and leave to rest while you cook the onions. Turn the hotplate heat up to high.

Drizzle a little extra oil on the hotplate. Use your hands to scatter the onions and garlic on the hotplate shaking excess marinade back into the bowl. Cook the onions for 10 minutes. During the cooking time, spoon over the reserved marinade and use some tongs to stir and toss the onion and garlic constantly until they are golden brown and limp looking. Serve with the pork chops and lime quarters.

4 pork chops,
about 2 cm (¾ in) thick
125 ml (4 fl oz/½ cup)
white rum
3 tablespoons
lime juice
125 ml (4 fl oz/½ cup)
pineapple juice
4 garlic cloves, peeled
2 large red onions,
finely sliced
1 teaspoon dried oregano
1 teaspoon dried cumin
1 teaspoon cayenne pepper
2 limes, cut in quarters

NEW YORK COWBOY

SERVES 4

**New York cowboy
spice rub**
2 teaspoons chilli powder
2 teaspoons Hungarian
paprika
2 teaspoons black
peppercorns
4 garlic cloves, crushed
80 ml (2½ fl oz/⅓ cup)
olive oil
2 teaspoons sea salt flakes

4 New York or sirloin steaks

A New York cut steak is also called porterhouse. It is a thick cut of beef, about 2 to 3 cm (about an inch), with a healthy layer of fat hugging one side. Like most people, I sometimes use the internet when I'm doing research. While I was looking at recipes I found a spice rub called New York cowboy spice rub. Intrigued? I was, especially when I read it asked for 6 tablespoons of salt in the mixture! Mental note, don't automatically assume the written word on the internet is gospel. If I had followed this I would have ruined some expensive meat. But, I do like the name of the rub so here is my version.

Put the chilli powder, paprika and black peppercorns in a spice mill and whiz together until the peppercorns are crushed and the mixture is powder-like. Put the powder in a non-metallic dish large enough to fit the steaks. Add the garlic and oil and stir around so you have a fiery red paste. Add the steaks and rub the paste all over them. Cover and refrigerate for 6 hours or overnight. Just remember to take them out of the fridge 1 hour before cooking. These are thick cuts of meat so they will need to come to room temperature, otherwise the steaks will still be fridge cold in the centre when you eat them.

Preheat the barbecue grill to medium. Sprinkle the salt on the steaks, put on the grill and cook for 6 minutes with the lid on. Turn over and cook for another 6 minutes. Wrap the meat in foil, turn the barbecue heat off and sit the meat on the warm barbecue lid for 5 minutes. Remove the meat from the lid and leave covered for another 5 minutes to rest before eating.

LAMB RACK MARGHERITA

All the flavours of a pizza on a rack of lamb? The marinade here is really a sauce, kind of like a tapenade, coating the lamb, keeping it moist and full of flavour. Anchovies with lamb may sound odd but the anchovies break down and act to season the meat.

For the marinade, put all the ingredients in a food processor and whiz until you have a chunky paste. You don't want this to be over-processed. Put the lamb racks in a non-metallic dish and pour the marinade over the meat, avoiding the bones. Sit the lamb in the dish so the bones point upward, cover and refrigerate overnight.

Remove the rack from the fridge 1 hour before cooking and season with sea salt and freshly ground black pepper.

Preheat the barbecue hotplate to high. Put two layers of foil on a cooking rack and sit the lamb on the rack. Sit the rack on the hotplate and cook for 15 minutes, until the cutlet bones start to char. Loosely cover the lamb with foil, reduce the heat to low and cook for 10 minutes. Turn the barbecue off and sit the rack on the hot lid for 10 minutes. Remove and allow to rest for another 15 minutes before carving.

2 tomatoes
3 garlic cloves, chopped
24 little black olives (in oil, not kalamata)
handful flat-leaf (Italian) parsley leaves
1 tablespoon oregano leaves
1 tablespoon olive oil
½ teaspoon freshly ground black pepper

2 milk-fed racks of lamb, each with 6–8 small cutlets

BEEF RIBS
WITH BARBECUE SAUCE

SERVES 4

Spice rub
1 teaspoon dried thyme
2 teaspoons smoked paprika
2 teaspoons chilli powder
½ teaspoon freshly ground black pepper

2 x 800 g (1 lb 12 oz) beef ribs, each with eight rib bones about 5 cm (2 in) long

Barbecue sauce
2 tablespoons brown sugar
2 tablespoons cider vinegar
150 g (5½ oz/½ cup) tomato sauce (ketchup)
1 tablespoon chicory
2 teaspoons mustard powder
1 tablespoon worcestershire sauce

Most of the recipes you see for any of these more traditional 'American-style' barbecue ribs will have you pre-cook the ribs in the oven before they make it to the barbecue. I am not sure I see the point of calling something a barbecue if it has spent more time in the kitchen! So be patient with these and you will be rewarded, as this version is cooked entirely on the barbecue. When I bought these ribs the butcher asked what I was planning on doing with them. When I told him my plan he declared that it would easily be a 'three tin number'. By this he meant three cans of beer and he was spot on!

Combine the spices for the spice rub in a small bowl. Put the beef ribs in a snug-fitting non-metallic dish and rub over the ribs. Cover and refrigerate overnight, turning often.

Remove the ribs from the fridge 1 hour before cooking. Wrap each rack in baking paper, then wrap in foil.

Combine the barbecue sauce ingredients in a bowl and set aside.

Preheat the barbecue hotplate to low. Sit the ribs on a rack and sit the rack on the hotplate. Cook for 1½ hours, turning often so the ribs steam in the paper. Unwrap the ribs and put them on the hotplate. Turn the heat to medium and start to baste. Brush the ribs with the sauce and turn over. Continue to baste and turn the ribs for 15 to 20 minutes, until all the sauce has been used and the ribs are very tender. Remove to a plate, cover with foil and rest for 10 minutes. Cut each rack in half and serve.

PERSIAN LAMB CUTLETS

Persian marinade
1 red onion, chopped
1 tomato, chopped
4 garlic cloves, chopped
1 teaspoon ground cumin
1 teaspoon allspice
1 teaspoon ground
cinnamon
½ teaspoon cayenne pepper
1 small bunch coriander
(cilantro), leaves only,
chopped

16 lamb cutlets

Mint yoghurt
185 g (6½ oz/¾ cup) Greek-
style natural yoghurt
2 Lebanese
(short) cucumbers
2 garlic cloves, crushed
handful mint, finely
chopped

Both lamb and pork can handle sweet spices. Like a few other recipes in this book, the Middle Eastern influence here is obvious. You could try this spice mixture on pork cutlets.

For the Persian marinade put all the ingredients in a food processor and whiz until well combined and you have a chunky-looking paste.

Put the lamb in a flat non-metallic dish and smear the paste all over them, cover and refrigerate overnight.

Remove the lamb from the fridge 30 minutes before cooking.

Preheat the hotplate to high and drizzle with a little olive oil to grease. Put the lamb on the hotplate and cook for 2 minutes on each side, so it is still pink in the middle. Cook for an extra 2 minutes each side for well done. You may need to adjust the temperature if cooking longer as the marinade will burn. Remove the lamb to a serving platter, cover and rest for about 5 minutes.

Meanwhile, combine the mint yoghurt ingredients and put in a bowl. (It's best to make this at the last minute because the cucumber will go soggy in the yoghurt if it is left to sit.) Serve the lamb cutlets with the mint yoghurt.

VIETNAMESE GARLIC, BLACK PEPPER AND LIME STEAKS

I really do reckon one of the best things about barbecuing is that it can easily incorporate bits and pieces of cooking from all over the world. This recipe uses Vietnamese ingredients, which are characteristically fresh and intense—perfect for marinades, where you really do need strong flavours to penetrate and linger in the cooked meat.

Peel the garlic and roughly chop. Sprinkle with a pinch of sea salt and begin to chop some more and crush with the side of the knife. The salt will break down the fibres in the garlic and allow it to be effectively crushed without losing half the clove like you do in a crusher. Put the garlic in a bowl with the fish sauce, oil, sugar, spring onions and black pepper.

Put a steak on a chopping board and use a sharp knife to carefully cut each fillet, cutting parallel to the chopping board, to make two pieces about 2 cm (¾ in) thick. Repeat so you have eight fillets. Put the meat into a non-metallic dish, pour over the marinade and rub all over the steaks. Cover and refrigerate for 3 to 6 hours, turning occasionally.

Remove the steaks from the fridge 30 minutes before cooking.

Combine the rice vinegar, lime juice and soy sauce in small bowl.

Preheat the barbecue hotplate to high with the lid on so it is really hot. Drizzle a little olive oil on the hotplate to grease and then add the steaks. Cook for 2 minutes, without moving or turning, so a golden crust forms. Turn over and cook for a further 2 minutes for medium-rare. Put the steaks in a bowl and pour over the lime sauce mix. Use some tongs to turn the steaks over to coat in the sauce, then serve.

Vietnamese garlic, black pepper and lime marinade
6 garlic cloves
1 tablespoon fish sauce
1 tablespoon olive oil
1 teaspoon sugar
4 spring onions (scallions), white part only, finely chopped
1 teaspoon freshly ground black pepper

4 thick beef fillet steaks, about 4 cm (1½ in) thick
1 tablespoon rice vinegar
1 tablespoon lime juice
1 tablespoon soy sauce

MERGUEZ SAUSAGES

Made with beef or lamb, these are little home-made sausages with a history originating in north Africa. The paprika gives them their unique redness. The tomato jam can be made a day or two in advance, kept in the fridge and served on the side with many of the other red meat recipes.

For the jam, preheat the barbecue hotplate to high. Put the tomatoes in a bowl with the chilli and olive oil and toss around. Put the tomatoes, cut side down, and chilli on the hotplate and cook for about 3 to 4 minutes, until they just start to develop a golden crust. Turn over and cook for another 3 to 4 minutes, pressing down with a flat metal spatula. Remove and put the tomatoes and chilli in a food processor while they are still hot with the garlic, sugar and a large pinch of sea salt. Pulse until really mushed up. Transfer to a small saucepan and boil until the mixture has reduced by about half, stirring often. This will take about 8 to 10 minutes. Add the honey and boil for another 2 to 3 minutes, until you have a red sauce the colour of a rich chutney. Put in a bowl and allow to cool.

To make the sausages, put the meat, spices and salt in a large bowl. Use your hands to combine, throwing the meat against the side of the bowl. Lightly grease your hands with olive oil and form the meat into sixteen balls about the size of a large walnut. Form them into small sausages about 5 to 6 cm (2 to 2½ in) long. Put them on a tray lined with baking paper. Cover and refrigerate overnight.

Preheat the barbecue grill to high. Lightly brush the sausages with some extra olive oil and cook for about 6 minutes, turning every couple of minutes until the meat is no longer pink. These are quite small so basically once they look cooked all over they will be ready.

Spicy tomato and honey jam
4 ripe tomatoes, cut in half
1 large red chilli (seeded if it is a really hot one), sliced
1 tablespoon olive oil
1 garlic clove, crushed
½ teaspoon sugar
90 g (3¼ oz/¼ cup) honey

750 g (1 lb 10 oz) minced (ground) beef
2 garlic cloves, finely chopped
1 tablespoon ground cumin
2 teaspoons ground coriander
1 tablespoon zatar mix (optional)
1 tablespoon paprika
1 teaspoon cayenne pepper
1 teaspoon dried thyme
1 teaspoon sea salt
extra zatar, to sprinkle on top

LAMB SHOULDER WITH ROSEMARY AND GARLIC

SERVES 4

1 shoulder of lamb, about
1–1.25 kg (2 lb 4 oz–
2 lb 12 oz)
1 garlic bulb
1 bunch rosemary
1 bunch thyme
3 tablespoons olive oil
12 baby potatoes (optional)

Not the prettiest cuts of meat, but pretty tasty nonetheless. Cold cuts can be made into a toothsome sandwich, smeared with tomato and honey jam.

Using a small, sharp knife, cut about 10 to 12 incisions in the skin of the lamb, about 1 cm (½ in) wide, but not going into the meat. Peel 2 garlic cloves and finely slice. Slide the garlic slices in under the skin of the lamb. Cut 3 to 4 cm (1¼ to 1½ in) lengths off the rosemary tops and use the knife to carefully slide these too under the skin with the garlic. Rub a generous amount of sea salt evenly over the skin of the lamb and leave the lamb to sit at room temperature for 1 hour.

Separate the remaining garlic cloves and put them, unpeeled, in a deep-sided baking tin with the remaining rosemary and the thyme.

Preheat the barbecue hotplate and grill to high and close the lid to create a hot-oven effect. Pour enough water to come halfway up the sides of the baking tin and sit a rack on top of the dish, making sure it is steady and even. Sit the lamb on the rack and drizzle the oil over the skin. Put the baking dish on the hotplate of the barbecue and cook for 30 minutes with the lid on. Within about 10 minutes you should hear the skin start to sizzle. After 30 minutes, add the potatoes if using, placing them around the shoulder. Turn the heat to low and cook for another 1½ hours. Check every 30 minutes or so, topping up with boiling water if needed and turning the potatoes. Remove the potatoes and keep warm, loosely cover the lamb with foil and cook for a further 30 minutes.

Remove the lamb to a large serving plate, cover with foil and rest for 20 to 30 minutes. Serve with the potatoes.

MIXED MEAT GRILL

I am not too sure what a mixed grill is exactly. I do remember seeing them on breakfast menus in the '70s in country motel restaurants; lots of bacon, sausages and steak with fried eggs. Actually, this is making me hungry! This is a slightly more posh version, using fillet and T-bone, but if the mention of bacon and sausage leaves you hankering then by all means add these. The eggs too if you like.

2 T-bone steaks
2 fillet steaks (quite thick, about 3–4 cm/1¼–1½ in), about 150 g (5½ oz) each
8 lamb cutlets
1 garlic bulb, cloves separated, left unpeeled
6 sprigs rosemary
1 small bunch thyme
3 tablespoons olive oil
3 tablespoons sherry vinegar
1 teaspoon freshly ground black pepper

Put the steaks and the cutlets in a snug-fitting non-metallic dish. Add all the other ingredients and toss everything together so the herbs and garlic are evenly distributed over, under and between the pieces of meat. Cover and refrigerate overnight, tossing a few times.

Remove the plate of meat from the fridge 1 hour before cooking.

Preheat the barbecue hotplate and grill to high. Now you will need a timer or some sort of stopwatch to make things easier here. All the meat is cooked medium-rare.

Put the fillets on the hotplate with some of the garlic cloves and herbs strewn about the meat and cook for 2 minutes, pressing down occasionally with a flat metal spatula but without moving or turning. When the fillet steaks have been cooking for 2 minutes, put the T-bones on the grill, again with some of the garlic and herbs, and cook both for 4 more minutes. Turn both the fillet and T-bone steaks over.

Cook for another 4 minutes, then remove the T-bone steaks to a heatproof plate, covered with foil. Cook the fillet steaks for another 2 minutes then put these too with the T-bones and cover. Cook the cutlets for 3 minutes on the grill then turn over and cook for another 2 minutes and add to the other meat. Turn the barbecue off and set the plate of meat, covered with foil, on the lid of the barbecue to rest for 10 minutes.

Serve the mixed grilled meats with an arrangement of sauces and condiments on the side.

BUTTERFLIED LAMB MASALA

Serves 6-8

Green masala marinade
1 tablespoon black
mustard seeds
1 tablespoon cumin seeds
1 tablespoon
coriander seeds
1 teaspoon turmeric
4 cardamom pods
1 cinnamon stick,
broken up
4 spring onions (scallions),
white part and a little of the
green finely chopped
4 garlic cloves
3 large green chillies
1 small bunch coriander
(cilantro), chopped
1 tablespoon finely
grated ginger
½ teaspoon ground
black pepper
3 tablespoons olive oil
3 tablespoons lemon juice

1 small leg lamb,
about 1.8 kg (4 lb),
butterflied

Do keep your eye on this one. It is thick in parts so it is not to be rushed, causing it to burn before cooking on the inside. Having said this, lamb is best pink. But if that is not your thing, cook on low heat for an extra 15 or 20 minutes. And let it sit on the hot barbecue lid for 20 minutes. The green masala marinade is a base curry paste that can be used in curries. Just fry off in a little oil, add some cubed lamb or beef, top with water and cook on a very low heat until the meat is fork tender.

For the green marsala, put the mustard seeds, cumin, coriander seeds, turmeric, cardamom and cinnamon in a small dry frying pan over high heat. Shake the pan over the heat until the mustard seeds pop and the mixture emits an aromatic smoke. Allow to cool then grind in a small spice mill (or mortar and pestle) to a rough powder. Put the spices in a food processor with the other ingredients, except the meat, and whiz to a chunky darkish-green paste. Remove to a bowl. This can be made in advance and kept in a non-metallic dish, covered in the refrigerator.

Cut 5 mm (¼ in) deep incisions on the skin side of the lamb about 5 cm (2 in) apart. This will help the lamb to cook more evenly, and allow the intense flavour of the marinade to penetrate into the meat. Put the lamb into a large, flat non-metallic dish with the marsala marinade and rub the marinade all over the lamb, making sure you rub into the incisions. Cover and refrigerate overnight, turning often.

Remove the lamb from the fridge at least 1 hour before cooking.

Preheat the barbecue hotplate and grill burners to high. Sit the lamb on a cooking rack and sit the rack over a roasting tray half-filled with water. Put the tray on the hotplate, cover with the lid and cook for 15 minutes. Turn all the burners to low and cook for a further 25 minutes. Cover with cooking foil and rest for 20 minutes before carving.

Next time: Rub the marinade over 4 chicken leg quarters. Allow to marinate for 3 to 6 hours and cook on a medium barbecue for 12 minutes on each side.

SPICY COUSCOUS STUFFED PORK

SERVES 4

Proof that necessity is the mother of invention. On a late and lovely Sunday afternoon in summer, with no desire to leave the house, I decided a barbecue was in order. The cupboards were almost bare. Thankfully, for some reason I always have a packet of couscous stashed in the depths of that awkward-to-get-at corner kitchen cupboard and a lone pork fillet in the refrigerator. I do like making couscous this way, dry-fried in the pan with aromatics to flavour, then water added as per the usual cooking technique. It makes for a really tasty, smoky-flavoured couscous, and worked a treat with the pork.

For the stuffing, put the couscous, cumin, paprika and chilli powder in a small frying pan and cook over high heat for 2 minutes, shaking the pan, until the mixture emits an aromatic smoke. Put the spices into a small bowl with the currants and butter. Add 125 ml (4 fl oz/½ cup) of boiling water, quickly stir, then cover for 10 minutes. Fluff with a fork and use your fingers to separate as many grains of couscous as possible, then stir through the pine nuts and coriander and season with sea salt and freshly ground black pepper.

Make a cut along the length of the pork fillets so the pork opens up, or butterflies. Spoon the couscous along the length of the pork then close. Tie each of the pork fillets with kitchen string and put in a snug-fitting non-metallic dish with the olive oil and lemon juice. Cover and set aside for 30 minutes.

Preheat the barbecue hotplate to medium–high. Remove the pork from the dish, sit on a plate or chopping board and sprinkle a large pinch of sea salt over each fillet. Put the pork on the hotplate and cook for 8 minutes, with the lid on, then turn over and cook for another 5 minutes. Lightly wrap the pork in cooking foil for 5 minutes, to allow to rest, then slice across the fillet into 1 cm (½ in) wide strips to serve.

95 g (3¼ oz/½ cup) couscous
½ teaspoon ground cumin
½ teaspoon smoky paprika
¼ teaspoon chilli powder
1 tablespoon currants
1 tablespoon butter
1 tablespoon pine nuts, lightly toasted
2 tablespoons finely chopped coriander (cilantro)
2 large pork fillets, about 400 g (14 oz) each
1 tablespoon olive oil
1 tablespoon lemon juice

ROAST BEEF

SERVES 6

4 garlic cloves, chopped
1 tablespoon thyme leaves
2 large handfuls flat-leaf
(Italian) parsley, roughly
chopped
1 teaspoon sea salt flakes
2 tablespoons olive oil
1–1.25 kg (2 lb 4 oz–2 lb
12 oz) roasting beef fillet,
with a nice thin layer of fat

Horseradish cream
185 g (6½ oz/¾ cup)
sour cream
1 tablespoon horseradish

How many recipes for roast beef have you come across? Or maybe you don't follow a recipe? Either way, the tricky thing about a good roast-beef meal is the timing. Many recipes are written forgetting that the home cook simply doesn't have enough space in the oven to cook the beef and the veggies at the same time and, if you are British, probably the Yorkshire puds too! You can cook a pretty close to perfect bit of beef on the barbecue, and why not serve it with barbecue-roasted veggies too and some horseradish sour cream?

Using a mortar and pestle, pound the garlic, herbs, salt and oil until you have a coarse paste. Rub all over the beef and set aside for 1 hour to come to room temperature.

Preheat all the barbecue burners to high, with the lid on, creating a hot-oven effect. Half-fill a roasting tin with boiling water and sit a rack on top, making sure it is steady and not going to fall off during cooking. Sit the roasting tray on the grill side of the barbecue.

Starting with the fat side down, cook the beef for 1 minute on each of its four sides on the hotplate, so it is just brown all over. Sit the beef on the rack, skin side up, close the lid and cook for 20 minutes, so the beef is just verging on dark brown in some places. Turn the barbecue off, wrap the beef in foil and then sit the beef on top of the hot lid for 15 minutes. Remove and allow to rest for another 20 minutes. While the beef is resting combine the sour cream and horseradish in a bowl. Carve the beef and serve with the horseradish cream.

FISH ESSENTIALS

Nothing typifies a casual approach to barbecuing more than cooking seafood. This chapter, titled 'fish', takes some poetic licence as fish means all the creatures of the sea, with or without fins, claws, shells and tentacles. It is cooking with life aquatic, Neptune's pets. It is fish cooked whole with crispy skin intact and served with flavours from all over the globe.

Barbecuing seafood is all too easy, and so it should be. In my book the biggest mistake with seafood is to overcook it. Fresh prawns really do need no more than a few minutes on each side, seared to curly pinkness. By the time you throw them on, they are almost ready to be taken off. Strips of cuttlefish cook in no time at all. Fish fillets can be wrapped in newspaper or banana leaves and steamed on the hotplate.

For fish, the barbecue is for creative cooking, using the barbecue in ways you didn't think possible. A sheet of baking paper is all that is needed to prevent the delicate skin and flesh of fish from sticking.

The hotplate can be used like an outdoor frying pan to cook up much-loved fish cakes, a classic Spanish romesco sauce, the celestial flavours of ginger and shallots, or the essence of a Greek taverna with lemon, salt and olive oil—lovely little marinated and grilled octopus.

It is superfluous to say fresh and seafood together. This should be a given. A visit to your local fish market or monger is in order. Prawns should be glossy and in blue and green hues of the ocean itself, firm with no blemishes. Fresh fish will have clear eyes and look wet and if you live in a warm climate they should be kept packed on lots of clean ice. Fresh fish won't smell fishy. It will smell like the ocean. And if you have ever smelt a fresh mussel, you know where I'm coming from.

LAKSA PRAWN SKEWERS

You will pretty much always find a jar of authentic laksa paste in my cupboard. Some say the word means 'ten thousand', which refers to the number of ingredients needed to make an authentic paste. So I do avoid making it myself. Good-quality pre-made pastes are available and they are used in coconut milk based soups, with thin rice noodles, chicken, fried tofu and bean sprouts and some fresh lime on the side to cut through the richness. The paste, made creamy with a little coconut milk and balanced with sugar and salty fish sauce is an easy marinade for big prawns and could all too easily be used to marinate chicken in. Then barbecued, of course.

125 ml (4 fl oz/½ cup) coconut cream
2 tablespoon good quality laksa paste
1 tablespoon fish sauce
1 tablespoon brown sugar
125 ml (4 fl oz/½ cup) coconut milk
6 limes, cut into quarters
24 large raw prawns, deveined

Put the coconut cream in a small saucepan and bring to the boil for about 5 minutes, until little volcanic-like pools form, bubbling as the oils separate from the liquids. Stir the mixture as the coconut cream darkens around the edge and boil for another 2 minutes until it looks curdled. Add the laksa paste and stir to combine. Add the fish sauce and sugar and cook for 1 minute. The mixture will look dark at this stage. Stir through the coconut milk and bring to the boil for a minute. Remove and allow to cool completely.

Put the prawns in a non-metallic dish, pour over the laksa marinade and toss around to coat the prawns evenly. Cover and refrigerate for 3 hours. Soak twelve bamboo skewers in cold water for 30 minutes.

Remove the prawns, reserving the marinade and thread two prawns onto each of the skewers with a lime wedge on the end.

Preheat the barbecue hotplate to high and drizzle with a little vegetable oil to grease. Put the skewers on the barbecue and cook for 2 minutes. Turn over and cook for another minute so they are pink all over. Start brushing the prawns with the reserved marinade, turn over and cook for 1 minute. Repeat once more so the prawns are looking really golden as the paste is cooked onto the shell. Serve with a bowl for shells, finger bowls and napkins.

GRILLED WHITING

serves 4

2 whole whiting,
about 450–500 g
(1 lb–1 lb 2 oz) each,
cleaned and gutted
2 tablespoons olive oil
2 teaspoons sea salt
lemon, to serve

Whether we cook for a living, cook for a family or we only cook on the weekend it is easy to forget the simple things. And this always strikes me as a little odd when it is the simple things that are the most important. Cooking doesn't get much simpler (or impressive) than this, and it's the type of dish— like a classic pesto sauce or chocolate cake—that fond food memories are made of.

Make a couple of slashes in each side of the fish. Put the fish in a baking tin lined with baking paper and lightly brush each side of the fish with about half of the olive oil, then sprinkle the salt evenly over the skin. Cover and set aside.

Preheat the barbecue hotplate to high. If you have grills, put them on too to get the heat really cranked up. Drizzle the remaining olive oil over the hotplate to grease. Put the fish on the hotplate and cook for 5 minutes with the lid on, without moving the fish so it develops an even, golden crust. Use a large metal spatula to quickly turn the fish over and cook for another 5 minutes without moving. The skin should be slightly crispy and the flesh firm yet succulent. One fish can be shared between two.

SHICHIMI TUNA
WITH WASABI CREME

Shichimi is a Japanese chilli spice mix and its name means seven flavours. The spice mix will vary, depending on where you are in Japan. Here is my version, not completely traditional, but it should be a hit with tuna lovers. It is best appreciated if the tuna is cooked rare, which will bring out the flavour of the spices. You can of course cook your tuna well done, but take note, its flavour will change significantly and may not entirely complement the spices. The aonori is a tricky ingredient to find—sold in glass jars and individual little bags, it can be found in good Asian specialty food supermarkets.

Combine the spices in a bowl and set aside.

Put the tuna steaks on a tray lined with baking paper. Evenly sprinkle the spice mix and a little sea salt over both sides of the tuna and set aside.

Put the yolks and sour cream in a bowl and whisk to combine. Very slowly add the oil, whisking constantly, to make a smooth creamy sauce. Stir through the wasabi until combined.

Preheat the barbecue hotplate to medium and drizzle with a little vegetable oil to grease. Put the tuna on the hotplate and cook for 2 minutes on each side until the spice mix is cooked, crusted and golden on the tuna. Serve with the wasabi crème.

Shichimi spice rub
1 teaspoon chilli powder
1 teaspoon chilli flakes
2 teaspoons freshly ground black pepper
1 teaspoon mustard powder
3 tablespoons white sesame seeds
2 teaspoons poppy seeds
2 tablespoons aonori (fine, dried seaweed flakes)

4 tuna steaks, about 200 g (7 oz) each

Wasabi crème
2 egg yolks
2 tablespoons light sour cream
200 ml (7 fl oz) light olive oil
2 teaspoons wasabi paste

WHOLE BABY TROUT WITH LEMON AND DILL

SERVES 4

2 x 500 g (1 lb 2 oz) trout, cleaned and gutted
1 lemon, very finely sliced
1 red onion, very finely sliced
1 bunch dill

The combination of ingredients here is not reinventing the wheel. But it is a much-loved favourite. The trick here is to cook the fish (as I do with much barbecued seafood) on a couple of sheets of greaseproof paper directly placed on the hotplate. The paper conducts all the heat off the hotplate without the delicate skin of the fish tearing or sticking.

Lay the trout on a clean work surface. Inside the cavity of each trout put 3 to 4 slices of lemon, a few slices of red onion, 3 to 4 sprigs of dill, another layer of onions and lemon, and season the outside of the fish well with sea salt and freshly ground black pepper.

Preheat the barbecue hotplate to high. Tear off two sheets of baking paper about the same size as the hotplate and put onto the hotplate. Lightly brush the paper with olive oil. Put the fish on the paper and cook for 8 minutes, with the lid on. Turn over and cook for another 5 minutes. Both sides of the fish should be dark golden and the skin crispy. One fish can be shared between two.

PIRI PIRI PRAWNS

Piri piri sauce
1 large red capsicum (pepper)
1 tablespoon white wine vinegar
1 tablespoon olive oil
2 large red chillies, seeded
2 garlic cloves

24 raw large prawns, peeled and deveined, leaving the tails intact

There has been a huge number of Portuguese-style fast-food chicken outlets opening in recent times. My dirty secret is I kind of like them, especially the day after the night before. Although, the origins of the chilli condiment is African, from Mozambique actually, which was a former colony of Portugal. I have made up my own here for these prawns, but the flavours also would work well with fish and chicken.

Put the capsicum in a hot oven and cook until the skin is blackened and puffed all over, or put the capsicum on a hot barbecue grill, turning often with tongs and cook until blackened all over, then put in a clean plastic bag until cool enough to handle. Peel and seed the capsicum, without being too fussy as the odd blackened bit will add flavour. (And don't rinse under water or you'll lose the flavour.) Put the capsicum in a food processor with the other piri piri ingredients. Whiz until you have a fiery red paste. Put in a bowl, cover and set aside until needed. This will keep in the refrigerator for a few days.

Put the prawns in a bowl and add the marinade, tossing them around to coat evenly. Set aside for 30 minutes.

Preheat the barbecue hotplate to high and drizzle with a little olive oil to grease. Cook the prawns for 2 minutes on each side, so they turn bright pink all over. Generously brush the prawns with any left-over marinade and quickly turn them on the hotplate so the marinade cooks just a little. Quickly remove the prawns and serve with lots of finger bowls and napkins.

RED WINE OCTOPUS

SERVES 4

The baby octopus here have heads no larger than a walnut. After preparing the octopus, cut any larger ones in half as the cooking time is quick smart. I have found that octopus does something tricky to the heat of the barbecue. It diffuses the heat very quickly and you are left with ockies that stew, not sear. So do have your hotplate really hot for this one.

Put the olive oil in a small saucepan over high heat and cook the garlic, onion, celery and carrot for 3 to 4 minutes, stirring often so the onion softens. Put the hot mixture into a food processor with the bay leaves, parsley, red wine and vinegar and whiz for a few seconds until you have a chunky-looking, rich-coloured liquid. Put in a bowl and allow to cool completely.

Put the octopus in a large non-metallic dish and pour over the marinade, rubbing it all over the octopus. Cover and refrigerate overnight, stirring often.

Remove the octopus from the fridge 30 minutes before cooking.

Preheat the barbecue hotplate to high. Shake any excess marinade from the octopus, put on the hotplate and cook the octopus for 2 minutes each side until it begins to darken. Remove the octopus, sprinkle with parsley, drizzle over the olive oil, season with sea salt and freshly ground black pepper, and serve with lemon wedges.

3 tablespoons olive oil
2 garlic cloves, chopped
1 small white onion, finely chopped
1 stick celery, finely chopped
1 small carrot, finely chopped
2 bay leaves
handful chopped flat-leaf (Italian) parsley
375 ml (13 fl oz/1½ cups) red wine
3 tablespoons red wine vinegar
16 baby octopus, cleaned
2 tablespoons extra flat-leaf parsley
1 tablespoon extra virgin olive oil
lemon wedges, to serve

HOTPLATE FISH CAKES

SERVES 4

Perfect for many occasions—on a Good Friday barbecue, for a non-meat, fish-eating barbecue guest ('a pescatarian') or something to serve up for kids that they will love. And they look good. The fresh salmon can easily enough be replaced with a small tin of salmon, well drained.

Bring a large saucepan of lightly salted water to the boil and add the potatoes. Cook for 12 minutes then add the salmon cutlet. Put the lid on and cook for another 3 minutes, so the salmon is now a soft pink colour. Drain both and allow to cool. When cool enough to handle, remove the skin and bones from the fish and roughly flake into a large bowl.

Roughly mash the potatoes and add to the salmon with all the other ingredients. Use a large spoon to stir the mixture so the salmon is broken up and spread evenly throughout the mix. Wet your hands with water and divide the mixture into eight equal portions. Roll into balls. Put onto a tray lined with baking paper and gently press down to make a slightly flattened pattie. Repeat to make eight patties. Cover and refrigerate for a few hours or leave overnight.

Remove your patties from the fridge 30 minutes before cooking.

Preheat the barbecue hotplate to medium and drizzle with a little vegetable oil to grease. Cook the patties for about 5 to 6 minutes, gently pressing down once or twice with a flat metal spatula, until they develop an even golden-coloured crust. Turn over and cook for another 5 to 6 minutes. Serve with lemon wedges and mayonnaise on the side.

2 potatoes, about 500 g (1 lb 2 oz), peeled and quartered
1 salmon cutlet, about 250 g (9 oz)
3 spring onions (scallions), white and a small amount of the green part, finely chopped
large handful flat-leaf (Italian) parsley, finely chopped
½ bunch dill, finely chopped
1 teaspoon sea salt
1 egg, beaten
40 g (1½ oz/½ cup) stale breadcrumbs

lemon wedges and mayonnaise, to serve

SALT AND PEPPER CUTTLEFISH

SERVES 4

5 large cuttlefish hoods,
about 150 g (5½ oz) each
3 tablespoons olive oil
3 garlic cloves, crushed
2 teaspoons dried
chilli flakes
2 teaspoons white pepper
2 teaspoons sea salt
1 small bunch coriander
(cilantro), finely chopped
lemon wedges, to serve

When it comes to food every day is a new one and a new lesson is to be learned. I recently discovered that cuttlefish is a sweet and tender creature when cooked on a really hot barbecue. Its flesh looks like a meaty, white hood and needs only the shortest of cooking times; leave to rest for a couple of minutes then toss with flavourings for a lovely, simple summer meal.

Put the cuttlefish in a non-metallic dish with the oil and garlic, and toss them around to coat. Cover and refrigerate for 1 hour.

Preheat the barbecue hotplate to high. Remove the cuttlefish from the marinade, shaking off any excess oil. Put the cuttlefish on the hotplate and cook for 1 minute on each side. They will begin to curl up, so use a flat metal spatula to gently press down to flatten. Put the cuttlefish on a chopping board and leave to rest for a couple of minutes. Slice into 5 mm (¼ in) wide strips and put into a large bowl with the chilli flakes, pepper and sea salt. Use a pair of tongs to toss around so the cuttlefish slices are evenly coated in the spices. Add the coriander, toss again and serve with the lemon wedges on the side.

LING FILLET WITH CHAMPAGNE, LEEKS AND DILL BUTTER

SERVES 4

1 leek
125 g (4½ oz/½ cup) butter
2 garlic cloves
1 small bunch dill,
finely chopped
handful flat-leaf (Italian)
parsley, roughly chopped
250 ml (9 fl oz/1 cup)
Champagne or a dry
sparkling wine
800 g (1 lb 12 oz) ling fillet

I didn't mean for this to sound as posh as it does but I do use the term Champagne loosely, although to some this is a sin. You could use a spoonful of the lime pickle butter (page 189) on this instead of the champagne butter and replace the dill with some chopped coriander.

Finely chop the white part of the leek and slice off 5 mm (¼ in) thick rings from the green and set aside.

Put about 1 tablespoon of the butter in a small saucepan over high heat. When the butter has melted and sizzling add the leek and cook for 2 to 3 minutes, stirring often so the leek softens. Add the garlic, dill and parsley and cook for 1 minute then add the champagne. Bring to the boil, then reduce the heat to a simmer until the liquid has reduced by half. Add the remaining butter to the pan and stir until the butter has melted. Put in a bowl and refrigerate until needed.

For the fish, tear off 1 large piece of baking paper and fold over to give double thickness. Place the leek rings down the centre of the paper and sit the fish on top. Spoon the Champagne butter down the length of the fish. Firmly fold the baking paper over to form a parcel and tuck the ends underneath to enclose the fish.

Preheat the barbecue hotplate to high.

Put the fish on the hotplate and cook with the lid on for 15 minutes. Remove to a platter and allow the fish to rest for 5 minutes before unwrapping and serving directly from the paper with the melted butter spooned over. The fish will be so tender you should be able to use a spoon to cut and serve it.

SEARED RARE TUNA WITH BAY LEAF AND LEMON

SERVES 4

This is an extravagance, no doubt about it. But if you are a fan of good quality tuna then you know where I am coming from. You don't need to mess around with this fantastic fish too much, but the biggest mistake is overcooking. Just sear it, keeping its flesh rare. I like to use a whole piece but you could also use smaller fillets.

2 x 400 g (14 oz) pieces sashimi-quality tuna
3 tablespoons olive oil
1 tablespoon light soy sauce (preferably Japanese)
1 tablespoon lemon juice
4 bay leaves
1 lemon, thinly sliced
Japanese soy sauce (extra) and wasabi, to serve

Put the tuna in a non-metallic dish and add the other ingredients. Cover and refrigerate for 3 hours, making sure you turn the tuna every so often.

Remove the tuna from the fridge 30 minutes before cooking.

Preheat the barbecue hotplate to high.

Remove the tuna from the oil and put on the hotplate with the bay leaves and lemon. These will cook and impart their flavour to the fish. Cook the tuna for 2 minutes each side so it sizzles quickly and cooks to a golden brown. Cut each piece in half or use a sharp knife to cut into fine slices, sashimi style. Serve with soy sauce and wasabi to dip in.

WHOLE SNAPPER
WITH GINGER AND SPRING ONIONS

SERVES 4-6

1 large, whole snapper, about 2 kg (4 lb 8 oz), cleaned and gutted
3 tablespoons Chinese rice wine
10 cm (4 in) piece ginger
1 bunch spring onions (scallions)
1 bunch coriander (cilantro), chopped
3 tablespoons light soy sauce
3 tablespoons chicken stock
1 teaspoon white sugar
3 tablespoons light peanut oil
1 tablespoon sesame oil
½ teaspoon white pepper

This is a classic Chinese dish usually all done in a restaurant kitchen. But it is all smoke and mirrors, as all you are doing is assembling. The celestial duo of scallions and ginger has heavenly status in Chinese cooking so honour them and only use the freshest. Again, a few simple barbecuing tricks here are the only prerequisites for a perfectly steamed fish.

Cut several diagonal incisions across the skin and flesh of the fish. Put the fish in a large non-metallic dish and pour over the rice wine. Cut the piece of ginger in half and cut one half into thin discs. Cut half of the bunch of spring onions into 10 cm (4 in) lengths. Put the ginger discs, spring onion pieces and half of the coriander in the cavity of the fish. Cover and set aside for 20 minutes.

Meanwhile, peel and cut the remaining ginger into thin matchsticks. Cut the remaining spring onions on the angle into similar sized pieces as the ginger. Set both aside. Combine the soy, chicken stock and sugar in a small bowl, stir to dissolve the sugar and set aside.

Preheat the barbecue hotplate to medium–high. Tear off two large sheets of baking paper and put these on top of two sheets of cooking foil. Sit the fish in the centre of the baking paper. Fold the sides of the foil to form a parcel, firmly enclosing the fish. Sit the fish on a cooking rack. Put the rack on the barbecue hotplate and cook for 20 minutes, so the fish cooks and steams in the parcel.

Remove the fish to a serving platter and leave the barbecue heat on. Pour the sauce over the fish then scatter over the ginger and spring onions. Put the light peanut oil and sesame oil in a small frying pan and sit it on the hotplate. When the oil is smoking hot pour over the fish then quickly scatter over the remaining coriander and white pepper to serve. This is a real event and can be done at the table creating a bit of drama and anticipation.

TOM YUM LIME LEAF
AND CORIANDER PRAWNS

SERVES 4

Cheating at its finest, I am a huge fan of authentic Thai tom yum paste, which means it must be made in Thailand! Please do avoid those brands which are trying to jump on the Thai bandwagon as we have finally embraced the fresh flavours of Thailand. So besides always having a big jar of tom yum paste in the fridge, ready to add the usual suspects for a quick and spicy soup supper, I now have one sitting near the barbie ready to use as a ready-made marinade and baste. This is really good, not to mention easy.

24 raw large prawns, peeled and deveined, leaving the tails intact
1 tablespoon tom yum paste
1 tablespoon lime juice
4 small makrut (kaffir lime) leaves, very finely shredded
1 tablespoon olive oil
handful coriander (cilantro), chopped
4 extra makrut leaves
1 lime, cut in half

Combine the prawns in a non-metallic dish with the tom yum paste, lime juice, makrut leaves, olive oil and the coriander, tossing the prawns around so they are evenly coated in the marinade. Cover and set aside for 30 minutes.

Preheat the barbecue hotplate to high and drizzle with a little vegetable oil to grease. Put the prawns and whole makrut leaves on the barbecue and cook for 2 minutes, drizzling or brushing with any of the left-over marinade. Turn over and cook for another 2 minutes, making sure the prawns are sizzling the whole cooking time and are turning pink all over. Squeeze the lime over the prawns and quickly turn the prawns over on the hotplate to coat in the juices and spices, cooking for another minute on each side.

Serve with finger bowls and lots of napkins.

BARBECUED SNAPPER WITH A RYE ROMESCO SAUCE

SERVES 4

Rye romesco sauce
4 ripe tomatoes, cut in half
1 large red chilli, seeded and thickly sliced
4 garlic cloves, sliced
50 g (1¾ oz/⅓ cup) blanched almonds
2 x 1 cm (½ in) thick slices rye bread, toasted and roughly torn
1 teaspoon smoky paprika
2 tablespoons red wine vinegar
handful chopped coriander (cilantro)
3 tablespoons extra virgin olive oil

4 x small snapper (about 300g/10½ oz each), cleaned and gutted
1 bunch thyme
3 tablespoons olive oil
3 tablespoons lemon juice
lemon wedges, to serve

A bit like pesto, this sauce comes in many shapes and sizes. From the fish-loving Catalonian region of Spain it is a rich emulsion of olive oil, tomatoes, chillies and spices. I use rye bread as I like eating it toasted for breakfast and always have some leftover. It lasts for ages and gives an extra nutty edge to go with the almonds.

For the romesco sauce, preheat the barbecue hotplate to high and drizzle with a little olive oil to grease. Put the tomatoes on the hotplate, cut side down. Scatter over the chilli and garlic and cook for 3 to 4 minutes, using tongs to turn the chilli and garlic but leaving the tomatoes. Remove the chillies and garlic from the hotplate. Turn the tomatoes over and cook for another 5 minutes until they are really soft and slightly charred.

Put the almonds in a food processor and whiz until they are finely chopped. Add the tomatoes, garlic, chilli, bread, paprika, vinegar and coriander to the food processor and whiz so they are all combined and chunky looking. With the processor on, add the oil in a steady stream until it is all incorporated and you have a thick red sauce. Put into a container, cover and refrigerate until needed. Just remember to allow the sauce to come to room temperature before serving.

Cut several diagonal, deep incisions across each side of the snapper and put into a large, flat non-metallic dish with the thyme, olive oil and lemon juice. Brush the marinade over the fish and into the incisions then leave to stand for 30 minutes.

Preheat the barbecue hotplate to medium. Tear off two sheets of baking paper about the same size as the hotplate and put onto the hotplate. Lightly brush the paper with olive oil, put the fish on the paper and cook for 8 to 10 minutes, with the barbecue lid on, until the flesh is golden brown. Use a flat metal spatula to quickly and carefully turn the fish over and cook for another 5 minutes, again with the lid on. Serve the fish with romesco sauce and lemon wedges on the side.

CUTTLEFISH WITH CHORIZO AND POTATOES

'Surf and turf' with Spanish flavours. You may want to just cook the chorizo part of this recipe. Chorizo is packed full of hidden spices and garlic, quite rich actually, so the red wine vinegar really does temper it a tad.

Put the cuttlefish hoods in a non-metallic dish with the olive oil, lemon juice and paprika, tossing the cuttlefish around to coat. Cover and refrigerate for 3 hours.

Make a quantity of hotplate wedges (page 213) and put them in a heatproof bowl. Sit them on a warm part of the barbecue away from direct heat.

Preheat the barbecue hotplate to high and drizzle with a little olive oil to grease. Cook the chorizo for 1 minute on each side, until lightly crisp and golden. Pour the beer and vinegar over the chorizo so the liquids sizzle as they hit the hotplate. Push the chorizo around on the hotplate to coat in the sauce and cook for 1 minute, until the liquids evaporate, then put in a large bowl.

Cook the cuttlefish on the hotplate for 1 minute on each side, drizzling over a little of the tasty marinade. Remove the cuttlefish and slice into 1 cm (½ in) wide strips. Add to the bowl with the chorizo, then add the potatoes and mint leaves, tossing around to combine. Put on a serving plate.

500 g (1 lb 2 oz) large cuttlefish hoods
3 tablespoons olive oil
2 tablespoons lemon juice
½ teaspoon smoky paprika
2 chorizo sausages, sliced
2 tablespoons beer
2 tablespoons red wine vinegar
1 quantity hotplate wedges (page 213)
handful small mint leaves

THAI STYLE
GARLIC PEPPER BARRAMUNDI

SERVES 4

Garlic pepper paste
2 teaspoons white peppercorns
2 teaspoons black peppercorns
8–10 garlic cloves, chopped
6–8 coriander roots, chopped
2 tablespoons sugar
3 tablespoons fish sauce

1 large barramundi, about 1.25–1.5 kg (2 lb 12 oz–3 lb 5 oz), cleaned, gutted and scaled
limes wedges, to serve

The pepper paste, with the sugar, gives the fish here a sweet, caramel glaze. But be warned, the sugar is also a curse. It will burn if the hotplate is too hot and if left for too long on the direct heat of the hotplate. So I keep the barbecue heat to medium and use baking paper—it keeps the fish from sticking and makes it easier to turn the fish over which is good as the glaze becomes molten hot.

Pound the peppercorns in a mortar and pestle until they are all crushed. Add the garlic and coriander and pound to a paste, add the sugar and fish sauce, and stir until the sugar is dissolved. Put in a bowl and set aside until needed.

Cut several diagonal, deep incisions across both sides of the fish and rub the paste into the cuts and over the skin.

Preheat the barbecue hotplate to medium. Tear off two sheets of baking paper slightly smaller than the hotplate. Lay the baking paper on the hotplate, put the fish on the baking paper and cook for 8 to 10 minutes, with the lid on. Turn over and cook for 5 to 6 minutes, (you could do with another hand here) with the lid on. The fish should be just cooked through to the bone and flake easily, and the skin will be a lovely dark caramel colour. Put the fish onto a large platter and serve with lemon wedges on the side.

MUSSELS
IN LIME PICKLE BUTTER

Mussels are big, mussels are bold and mussels are made to share. This is a toothsome number for four, with a very tasty and tangy lime pickle butter, which I have only recently discovered vary greatly in flavour. Some lime pickles leave me feeling like I have just sucked on a lemon, yet others I want to eat with cheese and crackers. Odd, I know. This butter can be used on just about any fish, white fish especially.

Put 1 tablespoon of the butter in a small saucepan with the spring onion, pickle, turmeric, ginger, garlic, lime juice and pepper and cook over a medium heat until the ingredients have softened and become aromatic. Put into a bowl and stir through the herbs and remaining butter until well combined. Cover and refrigerate until needed.

Remove the lime pickle butter from the fridge to soften.

To cook the mussels, preheat the barbecue hotplate to high. Put the mussels onto the hotplate, pour over some of the wine and cook for 2 minutes on each side with the lid on, until the mussels open. Discard any that do not. Put the mussels in a large bowl and spoon over the softened butter. Add the coriander. Use a large pair of tongs to toss the mussels around and serve.

Lime pickle butter
100 g (3½ oz) butter, softened
2 spring onions (scallions), chopped
1 tablespoon good quality lime pickle, chopped
½ teaspoon turmeric
1 teaspoon finely grated ginger
2 garlic cloves, crushed
1 tablespoon lime juice
½ teaspoon freshly ground black pepper
handful coriander (cilantro) leaves, finely chopped
handful mint leaves, finely chopped

2 kg (4 lb 8 oz) mussels, beards removed and scrubbed
125 ml (4 fl oz/½ cup) white wine
1 bunch coriander (cilantro) leaves and 2–3 cm (¾–1¼ in) stems, finely chopped

ADOBO COD

Adobo marinade
1 small red onion, chopped
1 large red chilli
2 garlic cloves, chopped
1 teaspoon finely
chopped thyme
handful flat-leaf (Italian)
parsley, leaves only,
roughly chopped
2 bay leaves
3 tablespoons olive oil
3 tablespoons white
wine vinegar

800 g (1 lb 12 oz) thick cod
fillets, cut into large 3–4 cm
(1¼–1½ in) chunks

I think we all know what cod is, but what is adobo? It is a Spanish word used to describe a dish, some say to be a national dish of the Philippines—usually using meat, but the flavours are so good with a meaty white fish. I have since tried this with monkfish (a great fish fillet to use in Moroccan tagines by the way) and it works a treat.

Put the onion, chilli, garlic, thyme, parsley and bay leaves in a food processor and whiz to a paste. Heat the olive oil in a small saucepan over high heat and cook the paste for 3 to 4 minutes, stirring often, until the onion has softened and the mixture is aromatic. Remove from the heat, stir through the vinegar, and allow to cool. Put the fish chunks in a non-metallic dish, pour over the marinade and toss the fish to coat. Cover and refrigerate for 3 hours, turning often.

Remove the fish from the fridge 30 minutes before cooking.

Preheat the barbecue hotplate to medium and drizzle with a little olive oil to grease. Cook the fish pieces for 3 minutes on each of the larger sides. (The fish pieces will have irregular shapes.) Remove the smaller pieces from the hotplate and cook the larger, thicker, more triangular shaped pieces cut from the centre of the fillet for an extra minute on each of the smaller sides. The marinade will have cooked to a slightly charred red paste coating the fish.

PARCHMENT BAKED WHITING WITH LEMON SALSA BUTTER

SERVES 4

Lemon salsa butter
125 g (4½ oz/½ cup) butter
large handful coriander
(cilantro) leaves and stems,
finely chopped
3 spring onions (scallions),
finely chopped
1 tablespoon finely
snipped chives
1 large green chilli, seeded
and finely chopped
2 tablespoons lemon juice

2 x whiting fillets, about
350–400 g (12–14 oz) each

It seems very '70s to wrap something in paper, usually white fish fillets, and cook in the oven. A delicate method for this rather delicate fish that translates well to the barbecue and made more contemporary with some green chilli and coriander thrown in. I use whiting here, but any firm white fish will do.

Put the butter in a small saucepan and cook over a low heat until just melted, but don't let the butter boil. Add the other lemon salsa ingredients, with a pinch of sea salt and some freshly ground black pepper, stirring for a minute or so to combine, then set aside to cool to room temperature. Put the butter in a bowl, cover and refrigerate until needed.

Tear off two large pieces of baking paper, large enough with room to spare to wrap a whiting fillet in. Sit a fillet in the centre of the paper and spoon over half of the salsa butter. Bring the two long sides of the paper together and firmly fold over a few times then twist the ends to seal. Tie each twisted end with kitchen string. Now sit each parcel in a large piece of cooking foil. Fold the edges of the foil to firmly seal and form a parcel.

Preheat the barbecue hotplate to high. Put the fish parcels on the hotplate and cook for 10 minutes, with the lid on. The fish will be white and flaky and can be eaten directly from the parcels. Serve a parcel between two people to share.

SWORDFISH WITH PAPRIKA, LEMON AND HERBS

Here's some oddball trivia to share as you fire up the barbecue. The swordfish is a fast creature. It is a fish which means it is cold blooded, of course. That is, except for its eyes! This cunning predator has evolved to have warm eyes which move faster and therefore better to see their prey with. And continuing on a whimsical note, there are records of stabbings with the 'nose' of a swordfish—which is a sinister twist as we usually enjoy them skewered, which you could do here.

4 swordfish steaks, each about 2.5 cm (1 in) thick
3 tablespoons olive oil
1 teaspoon paprika
2 tablespoons lemon juice
4 bay leaves
1 small bunch thyme
lemon wedges, to serve

Put the fish in a snug-fitting non-metallic dish. Combine the olive oil, paprika and lemon juice in a small bowl then pour over the fish. Add the bay leaves and thyme, and rub the marinade all over the fish, evenly distributing the herbs. Cover and refrigerate for 3 to 6 hours. Remove the fish from the fridge 30 minutes before cooking.

Preheat the barbecue hotplate to medium and drizzle with a little olive oil to grease. Remove the fish from the marinade, shaking off the excess, and put onto the hotplate with the bay leaves and thyme. (Cooking the herbs will bring out their unique flavour.) Cook the fish for 8 to 10 minutes. Use some cooking tongs to move the herbs around on the hotplate so they sizzle in the oil and cooking juices of the fish. Turn the fish over and cook for another 5 minutes. Unlike tuna, it's best for swordfish to be cooked all the way through. Serve with lemon wedges on the side.

CHERMOULA FISH CUTLETS

SERVES 4

I think I have harped on in a few recipes about how good north African flavours are for use in barbecuing—they are made for it. The essentials of this traditional rub are garlic, cumin, some sort of chillies and some sort of fresh herbage. Often, the seafood is rubbed and marinated in a chermoula then added to a simple, fresh tomato sauce for a seafood tagine. I have used big blue eye cutlets here but any white fish will do. The cutlets are a horse-shoe or oval cut, which is the cross-section of the fish, with that big bone down the centre.

Put the chillies, garlic and salt in a mortar and pestle and pound until you have a chunky paste. Add the olive oil, cumin, ground coriander and fresh herbs and keep pounding until you have an aromatic, green thick paste.

Put the fish in a non-metallic dish and rub the chermoula all over. Cover and refrigerate for 3 hours. Remove from the fridge 30 minutes before cooking.

Preheat the barbecue hotplate to medium. Tear off two sheets of baking paper about the same size as the hotplate. Put the baking paper on the hotplate and drizzle with a little olive oil to grease. Cook the fish for 5 minutes on each side until golden.

1 large red chilli, chopped
1 large green chilli, chopped
2 garlic cloves, chopped
½ teaspoon sea salt
3 tablespoons olive oil
½ teaspoon ground cumin
½ teaspoon ground coriander
large handful coriander (cilantro) leaves, roughly chopped
large handful flat-leaf (Italian) parsley leaves, roughly chopped
large handful mint leaves, roughly chopped
2 x blue eye cutlets (or cod), about 350 g (12 oz) each

HERBED SCALLOP SKEWERS WITH GREEN TABASCO MAYONNAISE

serves 4

Green Tabasco mayonnaise
2 egg yolks
2 teaspoons green Tabasco sauce
2 teaspoons fresh lemon juice
¼ teaspoon white pepper
125 ml (4 fl oz/½ cup) olive oil

24 large scallops, roe left on
2 tablespoons olive oil
2 tablespoons lemon juice
1 garlic clove, crushed
50 g (1¾ oz/½ cup) stale breadcrumbs
2 tablespoons finely chopped flat-leaf (Italian) parsley
1 tablespoon finely chopped oregano leaves
lemon wedges, to serve

I have a unique collection of Robert Carrier seafood recipe cards which acted as the inspiration for this. Everything old is new again. The crumbs could be used with prawns, white fish fillets or salmon. The green Tabasco mayo is a recipe staple—try it with the hotplate wedges (page 213) or on left-over barbecued-chicken sandwiches.

To make the green Tabasco mayonnaise put the egg yolks in a bowl with the Tabasco, lemon juice and a pinch of sea salt and white pepper. Whisk to combine and very slowly add the oil, whisking as you do. Start off by adding drop by drop then build up to a steady, constant stream, whisking all the time until the mixture looks like a thick custard. Put in a bowl, cover and refrigerate until needed.

Soak some bamboo skewers. Put the scallops in a non-metallic dish with the olive oil, lemon juice and garlic, and add some sea salt and freshly ground black pepper. Cover and refrigerate for 30 minutes. Thread three scallops onto the skewers to make eight skewers.

Put the breadcrumbs on a plate with the herbs and stir them around to combine. Lay one skewer at a time onto the herbed crumbs and roll them to lightly coat. Put the skewers onto a tray lined with baking paper.

Preheat the barbecue hotplate to high. Tear off two sheets of baking paper about the same size as the hotplate. Put the baking paper on the hotplate, brush with a little olive oil to grease, and then add the skewers. Cook for 2 minutes on each side so the crumbs are golden and the scallop flesh is still a little tender in the centre. Serve with the Tabasco mayonnaise and lemon wedges on the side.

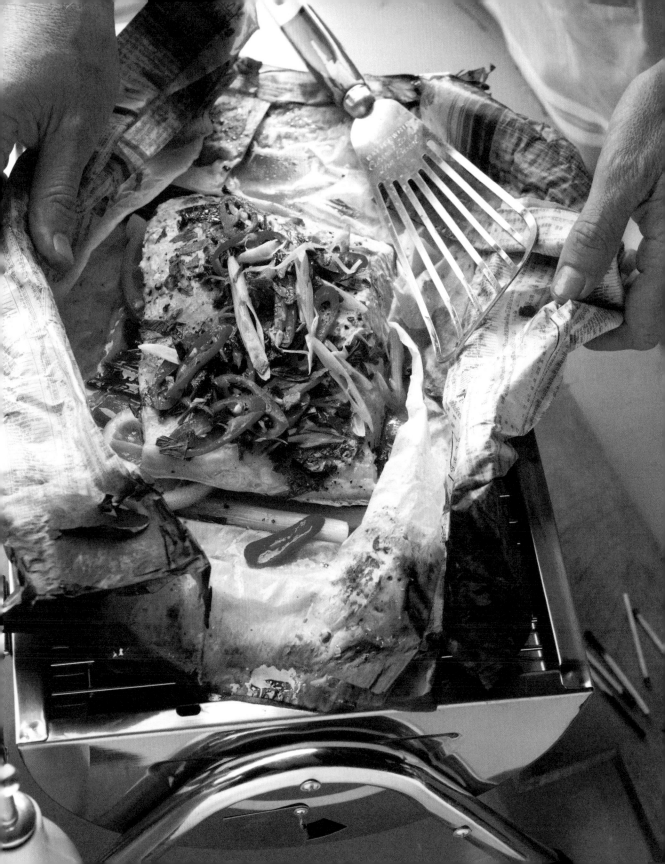

NEWSPAPER-WRAPPED SALMON WITH FRESH HERBS, LEMON AND CHILLI

Wetting the newspaper prevents it from burning on the hotplate (although it will a little anyway, which is fine) and creates a steamy environment for the fish to cook in. This makes cooking for a crowd too easy. Only limited by the size of your hotplate, you could easily cook six or eight of these and feed an army with little effort.

Preheat the barbecue hotplate to high.

Lay out two large sheets of newspaper on top of each other and liberally brush the newspaper all over with water to dampen. Tear off a piece of baking paper, slightly larger than a fish fillet and sit it in the middle of the newspaper. Repeat for the other fillet.

Finely slice 3 spring onions and put in a bowl with the other herbs and the chilli. Cut the remaining spring onions in half, lengthways, and lay these on top of the baking paper. Now lay the lemon slices on the spring onions. Sit the fish on the lemons and season well with sea salt and freshly ground black pepper. Scatter the herb mix evenly all over the top of the fillets. Combine the olive oil and lemon juice in a small bowl and pour over the fish. Fold up the newspaper to form a parcel by bringing the two long sides together, and folding down. Tuck the two shorter ends in underneath and sit the parcel, with the tucked sides on the hotplate. Cover with the lid and cook for 20 minutes. Remove and allow to rest for 5 minutes before carefully moving the fish to a plate. Drizzle over the cooking juices and serve.

2 x salmon fillets, mid cut, about 400 g (14 oz) each
bunch spring onions (scallions)
large handful flat-leaf (Italian) parsley leaves, roughly chopped
large handful coriander (cilantro) leaves, roughly chopped
1 handful mint leaves, roughly chopped
large red chilli, finely sliced (seeded if it's a hot one)
1 lemon, sliced
3 tablespoons olive oil
3 tablespoons lemon juice
1 teaspoon sea salt

GRILLED SUMMER VEGETABLES

SERVES 4

2 red capsicum (peppers)
2 fennel bulbs, thinly sliced lengthways
2 tablespoons olive oil
1 eggplant (aubergine), cut into thin rounds
1 large zucchini (courgette), thinly sliced lengthways
3 tablespoons light olive oil
handful flat-leaf (Italian) parsley, chopped
handful mint, chopped

This can be served warm, straight off the hotplate, or it can be one of those things for the super organised that can be made an hour or two before the barbecue has officially started. And it seems to benefit from this anyway, letting all the flavours come together. Add some fresh mint and crumble feta for a point of difference.

Preheat the barbecue grill to high. Put the capsicum directly on the grill and cook until the skin is puffed up and starting to blacken. Put into a clean plastic bag and allow to cool.

Meanwhile, brush the fennel with a little olive oil. Put the fennel on the grill and cook for 4 to 5 minutes on each side, until softened and striped with grill marks. Put into a large bowl. Brush the eggplant rounds with a little oil and cook for 3 to 4 minutes on each side. Place in the bowl with the fennel. Finally, brush the zucchini with oil and cook for 2 to 3 minutes on each side and add to the bowl with the other ingredients.

Peel and discard the skin of the capsicum. Pull out and discard the seeds. Roughly tear the flesh into strips and toss with the other vegetables. Season to taste with sea salt and freshly ground black pepper.

Good matches: Chicken with tarragon, olives and garlic, Turkey breast with herbed crust, T-bone Florentine, Veal cutlets with herbs and prosciutto, Pork shoulder with fennel and garlic, Roast beef, Grilled whiting, Piri piri prawns, Red wine octopus, Adobo cod, Swordfish with paprika, lemon and herbs, Chermoula fish cutlets.

See page 151 for recipe photograph.

MEDITERRANEAN SALAD

SERVES 4

I have to include a variation of the dressing for this salad whenever I can because it is one of my all-time favourites. It can be used as a dip, a dressing for grilled vegetables or as an accompanying sauce for lamb. Spoon over a classic mix of Mediterranean salad ingredients and you are all set for a memorable side for just about any barbecued meat.

Put the feta, garlic, dill, vinegar and olive oil in a food processor and whiz for a few seconds to combine. Add the milk in a steady stream with the motor running so you have a smooth and creamy sauce.

Put the salad ingredients in a large bowl and pour over the dressing to serve.

Good matches: Lemon chicken, feta and herb involtini, Minty salmoriglio lamb steaks, Lamb rack with feta and preserved lemon, Sheftalia, Veal cutlets with herbs and prosciutto, Fruity lamb fillets, Lamb rack margherita, Merguez sausages, Lamb shoulder with rosemary and garlic.

See page 83 for recipe photograph.

Creamy feta dressing
120 g (4¼ oz/1 cup grated feta cheese)
1 garlic clove, crushed
1 teaspoon dried dill
1 tablespoon white wine vinegar
125 ml (4 fl oz/½ cup) light olive oil
250 ml (9 fl oz/1 cup) milk

4 tomatoes, roughly chopped
2 Lebanese (short) cucumbers, cut into bite-sized chunks
black olives
1 iceberg lettuce, torn into large pieces
handful mint leaves

EASY BEARNAISE

SERVES 4

3 large egg yolks
1 tablespoon tarragon
vinegar
250 g (9 oz/1 cup)
unsalted butter
1 tablespoon finely chopped
tarragon
2 spring onions (scallions),
finely sliced

Does just seeing the words 'double' and 'boiler' send you running the other way? Yeah, I know we ought not dumb down cooking too much but if there is an easier way, just do it. And besides, food processors were not invented when many of the classic recipes were. Having said this, you do need a patient, steady hand when adding the hot butter to the eggs. This will keep in the fridge and is good cold. It does get tricky trying to reheat this without it doing weird things. But an old catering trick of mine is to store the sauce in a thermos and it will keep warm for a few hours.

Put the egg yolks and vinegar in a food processor and pulse a few times. Heat the butter in a small saucepan until it is bubbling hot and frothed, but do be careful it does not burn. While the butter is hot, and with the motor running, carefully start to pour the hot butter into the food processor in a steady stream until it is all incorporated. Put into a bowl and put plastic food wrap on top of the sauce. Cover with plastic wrap. Refrigerate until chilled and thickened and stir through the tarragon and shallots.

Good matches: Cab sav beef ribs, Veal cutlets with herbs and prosciutto, Pepper beef fillet, Steak with mushrooms, New York cowboy, Mixed meat grill, Roast beef.

See page 91 for recipe photograph.

SMOKY TOMATO RELISH

There isn't a better place to put food snobbery aside than at the barbecue. I was enjoying one of the best Good Friday barbecue get togethers at a friend's. As a starter to enjoy with drinks the hosts simply had plain corn chips with the best-tasting home-made dips—hummus, guacamole and a really fresh-tasting salsa. The salsa had all the usual suspects like tomatoes, coriander and red onion, but the flavour was something else. I was trying to pick what it was and was blown away when I was informed the secret ingredient was actually tomato sauce. And why not? Everyone has some.

4 tomatoes, not too ripe
4 garlic cloves
1 large red chilli
6 large spring onions (scallions)
1 tablespoon tomato sauce (ketchup)
large handful coriander (cilantro), roughly chopped

Preheat the barbecue hotplate to high. Put the tomatoes, garlic, chilli and spring onions on the barbecue and cook until the skins of each are evenly blackened, turning often. Remove them from the barbecue and set aside until cool enough to handle. You still want them to be warm though.

Remove the charred skin from the garlic, chilli and spring onions and roughly chop. Roughly chop the tomatoes, leaving their skins on as this gives the smoky flavour you are after here. Pound the garlic, chilli, spring onion, tomatoes and a good pinch of sea salt with a mortar and pestle until you have a chunky relish, and add the tomato sauce. Stir through the coriander just before serving.

Good matches: Beer-can roasted chicken, Blackened bird, Sheftalia, Spicy beef kebabs, Cheeseburgers, Topside steak sandwiches with balsamic onions and garlic crème, Merguez sausages, Mixed meat grill.

See page 142 for recipe photograph.

HERB-MARINATED POTATO SALAD

SERVES 4

16 small waxy potatoes,
cut in half
3 tablespoons olive oil
2 tablespoons red
wine vinegar
2 teaspoons mild mustard
4 spring onions (scallions),
finely sliced
handful flat-leaf (Italian)
parsley, finely chopped
small handful dill,
finely chopped

Always on the lookout for a potato salad, I am often drawn to those that are quick and easy. In my book, they are either creamy (mayonnaise-based) or, like this one, tossed with a vinaigrette and lots of fresh herbs. I like to let this one sit in its juices for a short while, so the potatoes are almost marinated and the herby flavour really permeates. Which makes it good to transport without refrigeration and, therefore, equally as good for a barbecue on the beach or in a park as it is in your own back yard.

Put the potatoes in a saucepan and cover with cold water. Cook on a high heat and as soon as the water boils, turn the heat off and cover the pan with a tight-fitting lid. Set aside for 20 minutes so the potatoes are cooked through but still firm.

Drain the potatoes, cut into large bite-sized pieces, and put into a large bowl. While they are still warm quickly whisk the olive oil, red wine vinegar and mustard in a small bowl until well combined. Add this and all the other ingredients to the bowl with the potatos as well as some sea salt and freshly ground black pepper. Use your hands to toss the potatoes around so each one is well coated in the herby sauce. Cover and set aside for an hour or so, stirring often, for the flavours to develop.

Good matches: Chicken with tarragon, olives and garlic, Beer can roasted chicken, Verdant chook, Lemon chicken, feta and herb involtini, Fino sherry chicken, Hungarian pork rack, Rump steak with ginger, garlic and soy, Fajita rump steak with mashed avocado, Mixed meat grill, Roast beef, Whole baby trout with lemon and dill.

See page 85 for recipe photograph.

COLESLAW

This is a popular recipe but a bit like apple pie in that everyone knows someone that makes the best version. For a good coleslaw you want it to be both creamy and crunchy without too much of an overbearing flavour so it can be eaten with just about all barbecued meats.

Put the cabbage in a colander and toss with the sea salt. Set aside for 30 minutes then rinse with cold water. Strain the cabbage thoroughly then use your hands to squeeze out as much liquid as possible and you will hear the cabbage crushing as you do. This will help to soften the texture of the cabbage. Put the cabbage in a bowl with the carrot and onion and toss to combine.

Combine the mayo, mustard, cream and horseradish in a bowl and pour over the cabbage mixture. Use tongs or your hands to combine the ingredients well. Serve as soon as possible.

Good matches: Beer-can roasted chicken, Verdant chook, Blackened bird, Fino sherry chicken, Hungarian pork rack, Hot dogs with beer-braised onions, Fajita rump steak with mashed avocado, New York cowboy, Mixed meat grill.

See page 41 for recipe photograph.

½ head red cabbage, finely shredded
½ head green cabbage, finely shredded
2 teaspoons fine sea salt
1 carrot, grated
1 small red onion, very finely sliced
250 g (9 oz/1 cup) whole egg mayonnaise
1 teaspoon mustard powder
125 g (4½ oz/½ cup) thick (double/heavy) cream
1 tablespoon prepared horseradish

HOME-MADE SWEET CHILLI SAUCE

SERVES 4

6 coriander roots and
4–5 cm (1¾–2 in) of the
stem, washed and chopped
4 garlic cloves, chopped
2 large red chillies, chopped
375 ml (13 fl oz/1½ cups)
white vinegar
440 g (15½ oz/2 cups) sugar

You would see this as nam jim on a Thai menu. The ingredients are all very easy to track down and the end result really is a very authentic-tasting sweet chilli sauce that can sit on the table in a bowl and be enjoyed by the spoonful!

Put the coriander roots into a pestle with the garlic, chilli and a generous pinch of sea salt. Pound until you have a murky-looking paste.

Put the vinegar and sugar in a saucepan with 375 ml (13 fl oz/ 1½ cups) of water and bring to the boil, stirring until the sugar has dissolved. Add the paste and reduce the heat to a steady but rapid simmer for 10 to 15 minutes, until the sauce is syrupy. Pour into jars and allow to cool.

This sauce will keep in the fridge for a couple of days.

Good matches: Thai barbecued chicken, Beer can roasted chicken, Quails with peanuts and Thai herbs, Penang beef satay, Vietnamese garlic, black pepper and lime steaks, Whole snapper with ginger and spring onions, Tom yum lime leaf and coriander prawns, Thai-style garlic pepper barramundi, Newspaper wrapped salmon with fresh herbs, lemon and chilli, Hotplate wedges.

See page 69 for recipe photograph.

HOTPLATE WEDGES

SERVES 4

We all love hot potato chips. Don't be tempted to constantly turn these on the hotplate. Just let them rest and sizzle letting them do their thing and get a golden skin. You can put cooked wedges in a metal mixing bowl and sit this on another part of the barbecue to keep warm while cooking your beast, bird or fish to serve them with. If you haven't already, as a simple shared snack with beer, try these dunked into a mixture of sour cream and sweet chilli sauce.

6 potatoes, such as desiree
2 tablespoons light olive oil
1 tablespoon celery salt or Cajun spice mix

Peel the potatoes and cut each into 6 to 8 wedges. Put the potatoes in a saucepan of boiling water, cover the pan with a lid and turn off the heat. Allow the potatoes to sit in the water for 10 minutes. Drain well and put the potatoes on a clean tea towel (dish towel) to dry and cool.

Preheat the barbecue hotplate to high. Put the potatoes in a bowl with 1 tablespoon of oil and the celery salt and toss to coat the wedges in the oil. Drizzle the remaining oil over the hotplate. Cook on the barbecue for 5 to 6 minutes, without turning or moving, until they look dark golden. Turn over and cook for another 3 to 4 minutes. Add the celery salt or spice mix and sea salt to taste.

Good matches: Barbecue chicken with green olive salsa verde, Beer-can roasted chicken, Blackened bird, T-bone Florentine, Cab sav beef ribs, Fajita rump steak with mashed avocado, Pepper beef fillet, Fillet steak with Café de Paris butter, Mustard and coriander lamb steaks, Cheeseburgers, Steak with mushrooms, New York cowboy, Mixed meat grill, Cuttlefish with chorizo and potatoes, Chermoula fish cutlets, Home-made sweet chilli sauce.

See page 91 for recipe photograph.

CUBAN BARBECUED CORN

serves 4

4 really fresh corn cobs
2 tablespoons softened
butter
2 tablespoons whole-egg
mayonnaise
50 g (1¾ oz) finely grated
manchega cheese
2 limes, halved

We all have one of these stories. I was taken to a very cool little diner in New York that specialises in Cuban barbecues and grills. The house speciality was corn on the cob, simply grilled. Just an ear of corn barbecued until dark golden and caramelised, the kernels about to burst out of their skins, then sprinkled with a Mexican cheese and some lime juice squeezed over. The cheese mostly used is cotija, or 'parmesan of mexico'. This cheese is hard to find out of North America, so you could use a manchega, available from a good deli and if you can't find that a good quality parmesan will do. By the way this cheese is really good on pasta. Aye carumba!

Preheat the barbecue grill to high. Put the corn on the grill and cook for about 12 to 15 minutes, turning often so they cook really dark golden—almost like a coffee colour around the edges. In the last minute or two of cooking, brush each cob evenly all over with the butter. Put on a serving plate. Spread some mayonnaise on each cob, sprinkle over the cheese and squeeze over the lime to taste.

Good matches: Chilli chicken BLT, Beer-can roasted chicken, Teriyaki and mustard chicken, Blackened bird, Chimichurri chook, Mexican pesto chicken, T-bone Florentine, Fajita rump steak with mashed avocado, Pepper beef fillet, Fillet steak with Café de Paris butter, Havana spiced pork chops with orange sherry onions, New York cowboy, Beef ribs with barbecue sauce, Mixed meat grill.

See page 45 for recipe photograph.

POTATOES IN THEIR JACKETS WITH SOUR CREAM AND CHIVES

SERVES 4

I run the risk here of stating the obvious but why not? There is nothing like potato, foil wrapped with a crispy bottom sitting in a pool of hot butter. Again, the trick though is patience and timing. A good roasted potato does take time, so don't throw them on at the last minute and expect a great spud.

4 large desiree potatoes, about 200 g (7 oz) each
60 g (2¼ oz/¼ cup) butter
125 g (4½ oz/½ cup) sour cream
2 tablespoons finely snipped chives

Put the potatoes in a large saucepan of boiling water. Cover and immediately turn off the heat. Leave the potatoes in the water for 20 minutes then drain. Cut the potatoes through the centre, to about 2 cm (¾ in) from the bottom. Then make another similar cut to form a cross. Put 1 tablespoon of butter on top of each potato with a little sea salt sprinkled on top. Potatoes love salt. Wrap each potato in foil, so the cut and buttered end is facing up and make sure it is well sealed. Repeat so each potato has a double layer of foil.

Preheat the barbecue hotplate to medium and sit a cooking rack (one from your oven is ideal) on the hotplate. Sit the potatoes on the rack, keeping the sealed side up. Cook for 1 hour. Towards the end of the cooking time you should hear the potatoes sizzling away inside their foil blankets. Remove and leave the potatoes in the foil for another 15 to 20 minutes before unwrapping.

Combine the sour cream and chives in a bowl. Unwrap the potatoes, and fill with the sour cream and chives.

Good matches: Chicken with tarragon, olives and garlic, Beer-can roasted chicken, Turkey breast with herbed crust, Veal cutlets with rosemary, anchovy and red wine, Hungarian pork rack, T-bone Florentine, Veal cutlets with herbs and prosciutto, Fillet steak with Café de Paris butter, Cheeseburgers, Steak with mushrooms, New York cowboy, Lamb rack margherita, Beef ribs with barbecue sauce, Lamb shoulder with rosemary and garlic, Mixed meat grill, Roast beef.

See page 62 for recipe photograph.

GARLIC BREAD

3 garlic cloves
125 g (4½ oz/½ cup) butter, softened
1 baguette, about 40 cm (16 in) long
2 tablespoons finely chopped flat-leaf (Italian) parsley

Garlic bread has had a hard time shaking free of its '70s fine-dining stigma. Garlic bread is really a humble side but do use good-quality ingredients; a baguette from a local artisan baker and do go all out with good-quality butter. You will taste the difference.

Peel the garlic and roughly chop. Sprinkle with a little salt and begin to finely chop and crush the garlic with the flat side of the knife. (The salt acts as an abrasive and breaks down the fibres in the garlic.) When the garlic is finely chopped and combined, put it in a bowl with the butter and parsley and stir to combine.

Preheat the barbecue grill to medium. Cut the baguette into 10 cm (4 in) pieces, then cut each in half. Spread the butter into each slice and firmly wrap the baguette in two layers of cooking foil. Put onto the barbecue with the lid down and cook for 10 minutes.

Good matches: Chicken with tarragon, olives and garlic, Beer-can roasted chicken, T-bone Florentine, Cab sav beef ribs, Pepper beef fillet, New York cowboy, Beef ribs with barbecue sauce, Mixed meat grill.

See page 102 for recipe photograph.

CHILLI BACON FRIED RICE

I take the cue for this from the great tradition of Japanese tepanyaki—sitting around those big hotplates as the chefs weave their magic, cooking everything on the hotplate including fried rice. This will go with all the barbecued food in this book that has Asian flavours, and there are heaps of these.

Preheat the barbecue hotplate to high and drizzle with a little light olive oil to grease. Quickly add the bacon, garlic, spring onion and chilli and start to stir-fry the ingredients together like you would in a wok or frying pan. Cook until the garlic just starts to brown. Use your hands to scatter the rice evenly all over the hotplate then drizzle any remaining oil over the rice, letting it sizzle for 5 minutes. (If you have one of those barbecue hotplates with a hole in the middle then use a non-stick roasting tray to sit on the hotplate.) Now start to turn the rice, using a wok charn or egg flip, and continue doing this for 5 minutes. Combine the soy sauce and sugar in a small bowl and stir to dissolve the sugar. Pour over the rice, so it sizzles and stir-fry for 1 minute. Stir through the coriander, basil and white pepper, and serve.

Good matches: Honey hoi sin chicken wings, Lemon thyme chicken wings, Teriyaki and mustard chicken, Green curry chicken, Sweet chilli and ginger chicken, Penang beef satay, Rump steak with ginger, garlic and soy, Chinatown pork, Vietnamese garlic, black pepper and lime steaks, Whole snapper with ginger and spring onions, Tom yum lime leaf and coriander prawns, Thai style garlic pepper barramundi, Newspaper-wrapped salmon with fresh herbs, lemon and chilli.

See page 56 for recipe photograph.

3 tablespoons light olive oil
2 bacon slices, finely sliced
3 garlic cloves, chopped
4 spring onions (scallions), chopped
2 large red chillies, seeded and sliced
750 g (1 lb 10 oz/4 cups) cooked long-grain rice
3 tablespoons light soy sauce
1 teaspoon caster sugar
2 large handfuls coriander (cilantro) leaves and stems, chopped
2 large handfuls Thai basil leaves, chopped
1 teaspoon white pepper

INDEX

adobo cod 190
Amelia's quail 29

balsamic onions 120
barbecue sauce 134
barbecues, types 8–9
barramundi, Thai style garlic pepper 186
baste, chilli caramel 36
béarnaise, easy 206
beef 67
  beef ribs with barbecue sauce 134
  cab sav beef ribs 90
  cheeseburgers 119
  fajita rump steak with mashed avocado 99
  fillet steak with café de Paris butter 115
  Merguez sausages 139
  mixed meat grill 143
  New York cowboy 128
  Penang beef satay 68
  pepper beef fillet 102
  roast beef 150
  rump steak with ginger, garlic and soy 84
  spicy beef kebabs 109
  steak with mushrooms 124
  T-bone Florentine 79
  topside steak sandwiches with balsamic onions and garlic crème 120
  Vietnamese garlic, black pepper and lime steaks 137
beer-can roasted chicken 32
Berber butter rub 93

Berber lamb 93
blackened bird 44
brining 19
butterflied lamb marsala 146
butters
  café de Paris 115
  lemon salsa 194
  lime pickle 189

cab sav beef ribs 90
café de Paris butter 115
Cajun rub 44
char siu glaze 105
cheeseburgers 119
chermoula fish cutlets 197
chicken
  barbecue chicken with green olive salsa verde 19
  beer-can roasted chicken 32
  chicken with tarragon, olives and garlic 26
  chilli caramel chicken 36
  chilli chicken BLT 22
  chimichurri chook 53
  fino sherry chicken 61
  green curry chicken 54
  harissa chicken 58
  honey hoi sin chicken wings 16
  lemon chicken, feta and herb involtini 50
  lemon soy roast chicken 21
  lemon thyme chicken wings 30
  lemongrass and lime leaf chicken 37
  Mexican pesto chicken 60
  sweet chilli and ginger chicken 55

teriyaki and mustard chicken 39
Thai barbecued chicken 20
verdant chook 40
chickens 15
chilli
    chilli bacon fried rice 217
    chilli caramel chicken 36
    chilli chicken BLT 22
    chilli pesto 60
    home-made sweet chilli sauce 212
    newspaper-wrapped salmon with
        fresh herbs, lemon and chilli 201
    sweet chilli and ginger chicken 55
chimichurri chook 53
Chinatown pork 105
chorizo with cuttlefish and potatoes
    185
cod, adobo 190
coleslaw 211
coriander
    coriander and pepper rub 20
    home-made sweet chilli sauce 212
    mustard and coriander lamb steaks
        116
    tom yum lime leaf and coriander
        prawns 179
corn, Cuban barbecued 214
couscous, spicy couscous stuffed
    pork 149
Cuban barbecued corn 214
curry, green curry chicken 54
cuttlefish
    cuttlefish with chorizo and
        potatoes 185
    salt and pepper cuttlefish 172

dill
    ling fillet with Champagne, leeks
        and dill butter 174
    whole baby trout with lemon and
        dill 164
dressings
    creamy feta 205
    garlic crème 120
    green Tabasco mayonnaise
        198
    horseradish cream 150
wasabi crème 163
duck with saffron rice stuffing and
    roasted veggies 46

fajita rump steak with mashed
    avocado 99
fennel, pork shoulder with fennel
    and garlic 110
fillet steak with café de Paris butter
    115
fino sherry chicken 61
fish 155
fish cakes, hotplate 171
fried rice, chilli bacon 217
fruity lamb fillets 125

garlic
    garlic bread 216
    garlic crème 120
    garlic pepper paste 186
    lamb shoulder with rosemary and
        garlic 140
    rump steak with ginger, garlic and
        soy 84

Thai style garlic pepper
    barramundi 186
topside steak sandwiches with
    balsamic onions and garlic crème
    120
Vietnamese garlic, black pepper
    and lime steaks 137
ginger
    rump steak with ginger, garlic and
        soy 84
    sweet chilli and ginger chicken 55
    whole snapper with ginger and
        spring onions 176
glaze, char siu 105
green curry chicken 54
green marsala marinade 146
green Tabasco mayonnaise 198

ham, Christmas barbecued glazed 94
harissa chicken 58
Havana spiced pork chops with
    orange sherry onions 127
herbs
    herb crust 63
    herb marinade 40
    herb-marinated potato salad 210
    herbed scallop skewers with green
        Tabasco mayonnaise 198
    newspaper-wrapped salmon with
        fresh herbs, lemon and chilli 201
    quails with peanuts and Thai herbs
        43
    turkey breast with herbed crust 63
    veal cutlets with herbs and
        prosciutto 101

honey hoi sin chicken wings 16
horseradish sour cream 150
hot dogs with beer-braised-onions 89
hotplate wedges 213
Hungarian pork rack 76

involtini, lemon chicken, feta and herb 50

jam, spicy tomato and honey 139
jerk lamb chops 98
jerk paste 98

kebabs, spicy beef 109

laksa paste 157
laksa prawn skewers 157
lamb 67
    Berber lamb 93
    butterflied lamb marsala 146
    fruity lamb fillets 125
    jerk lamb chops 98
    lamb rack with feta and preserved lemon 80
    lamb rack margherita 131
    lamb shoulder with rosemary and garlic 140
    minty salmoriglio lamb steaks 71
    mixed meat grill 143
    mustard and coriander lamb steaks 116
    Persian lamb cutlets 136
    sheftalia 81
    tandoori rack of lamb 106
lemon
    lemon chicken, feta and herb involtini 50
    lemon salsa butter 194
    lemon soy roast chicken 21
    lemon thyme chicken wings 30
    lemon thyme marinade 30
lemongrass 37
lemongrass and lime leaf chicken 37
lime pickle butter 189
ling fillet with Champagne, leeks and dill butter 174

marinades
    adobo 190
    fajita 99
    ginger soy 84
    green marsala 146
    herb 40
    hoi sin honey 16
    lemon thyme 30
    lemongrass and lime leaf 37
    Penang satay 68
    Persian 136
    sweet chilli 55
    Vietnamese garlic, black pepper and lime 137
meat 67
    mixed meat grill 143
Mediterranean salad 205
Merguez sausages 139
Mexican pesto chicken 60
mint yoghurt 136
minty salmoriglio lamb steaks 71
mussels in lime pickle butter 189
mustard and coriander lamb steaks 116

New York cowboy 128

octopus, red wine 167
olives
    chicken with tarragon, olives and garlic 26
    green olive salsa verde 19
onions
    Havana spiced pork chops with orange sherry onions 127
    topside steak sandwiches with balsamic onions and garlic crème 120
    whole snapper with ginger and spring onions 176
oregano, minty salmoriglio lamb steaks 71

pastes see rubs/pastes
Penang beef satay 68
pepper beef fillet 102
Persian lamb cutlets 136

pesto
    chilli 60
    Thai 43
piri piri prawns 166
pork 67
    Chinatown pork 105
    Havana spiced pork chops with orange sherry onions 127
    Hungarian pork rack 76
    pork shoulder with fennel and garlic 110
    spare ribs with black pepper and honey 70
    spicy couscous stuffed pork 149
potatoes
    cuttlefish with chorizo and potatoes 185
    herb-marinated potato salad 210
    hotplate wedges 213
    potatoes in their jackets with sour cream and chives 215
prawns
    laksa prawn skewers 157
    piri piri prawns 166
    tom yum lime leaf and coriander prawns 179

quails
    Amelia's quail 29
    quails with peanuts and Thai herbs 43

red wine octopus 167
relish, smoky tomato 207
rosemary
    lamb shoulder with rosemary and garlic 140
    veal cutlets with rosemary, anchovy and red wine 75
rubs/pastes
    for beef ribs 134
    Berber butter rub 93
    Cajun rub 44
    chermoula 197
    coriander and pepper 20
    garlic pepper paste 186
    green curry 54

jerk paste 98
New York cowboy 128
shichimi 163
tandoori 106
rump steak with ginger, garlic and
    soy 84
rye romesco sauce 180

saffron rice stuffing 46
salads
    coleslaw 211
    herb-marinated potato salad 210
    Mediterranean salad 205
salmon, newspaper-wrapped, with
    fresh herbs, lemon and chilli 201
salsa verde, green olive 19
salt and pepper cuttlefish 172
satay, Penang beef 68
sauces
    barbecue 134
    easy béarnaise 206
    piri piri 166
    rye romesco 180
    sweet chilli, home-made 212
    teriyaki and beer 39
seafood 155
    adobo cod 190
    barbecued snapper with a rye
        romesco sauce 180
    chermoula fish cutlets 197
    cuttlefish with chorizo and
        potatoes 185
    grilled whiting 158
    herbed scallop skewers with green
        Tabasco mayonnaise 198
    hotplate fish cakes 171
    laksa prawn skewers 157
    ling fillet with Champagne, leeks
        and dill butter 174
    mussels in lime pickle butter 189
    newspaper-wrapped salmon with
        fresh herbs, lemon and chilli 201
    parchment-baked whiting with
        lemon salsa butter 194
    piri piri prawns 166
    red wine octopus 167
    salt and pepper cuttlefish 172

seared rare tuna with bay leaf and
    lemon 175
shichimi tuna with wasabi crème
    163
swordfish with paprika, lemon and
    herbs 195
Thai style garlic pepper
    barramundi 186
tom yum lime leaf and coriander
    prawns 179
whole baby trout with lemon and
    dill 164
whole snapper with ginger and
    spring onions 176
sheftalia 81
shichimi tuna with wasabi crème
    163
skewers
    chimichurri chook 53
    herbed scallop skewers with green
        Tabasco mayonnaise 198
    laksa prawn skewers 157
    spicy beef kebabs 109
smoky tomato relish 207
snapper
    barbecued, with a rye romesco
        sauce 180
    whole, with ginger and spring
        onions 176
spare ribs with black pepper and
    honey 70
spatchcock, blackened bird 44
spice mix
    harissa 58
    Hungarian 76
spice rubs see rubs/pastes
spicy beef kebabs 109
spicy couscous stuffed pork 149
spicy tomato and honey jam 139
steak with mushrooms 124
stuffing
    saffron rice 46
    spicy couscous 149
sweet chilli and ginger chicken 55
sweet chilli sauce, home-made 212
swordfish with paprika, lemon and
    herbs 195

T-bone Florentine 79
tandoori paste 106
tandoori rack of lamb 106
tarragon, chicken with tarragon,
    olives and garlic 26
teriyaki and beer sauce 39
teriyaki and mustard chicken 39
Thai barbecued chicken 20
Thai pesto 43
Thai style garlic pepper barramundi
    186
tom yum lime leaf and coriander
    prawns 179
tom yum paste 179
tomato relish, smoky 207
topside steak sandwiches with
    balsamic onions and garlic crème
    120
trout, whole baby, with lemon and
    dill 164
tuna
    seared rare tuna with bay leaf and
        lemon 175
    shichimi tuna with wasabi crème
        163
turkey breast with herbed crust 63

veal
    hot dogs with beer-braised onions
        89
    veal cutlets with herbs and
        prosciutto 101
    veal cutlets with rosemary,
        anchovy and red wine 75
vegetables
    Cuban barbecued corn 214
    grilled summer vegetables 204
    see also potatoes; salads
verdant chook 40
Vietnamese garlic, black pepper and
    lime steaks 137

wasabi crème 163
whiting
    grilled 158
    parchment-baked, with lemon
        salsa butter 194

THANKS

It is an honour to be asked to work on a project like this, even more so with the team at Murdoch Books. For her tireless support and positive attitude and never ever (not even once!) not replying to an email, even when my ideas are way off the mark—thanks Kay, for making time and space for all of us with ideas, and for passing this one on to me. To the others who I don't see much of these days. To Juliet and the team who are tireless in producing beautiful books. Thanks to Emma, dotting the t's and crossing the i's, and for generally being very patient and supportive, and for organising a great project. To dear Jane, my beacon of food knowledge, I bow to you and have utmost respect for you. On the creative side, Reuben. Hope you get another award for this one! And to the team at photography, Brett and Lynsey—beautiful work. It went by too quickly!

Finishing on a personal note, this one is for Chris F-N. Thanks mate for instilling the unconditional confidence in me (and being a bloody talented man with the barbecue!).

Ta, lovelies.

Ross x

Published in 2008 by Murdoch Books Pty Limited

Murdoch Books Australia
Pier 8/9, 23 Hickson Road
Millers Point NSW 2000
Phone: +61 (0) 2 8220 2000
Fax: +61 (0) 2 8220 2558
www.murdochbooks.com.au

Murdoch Books UK Limited
Erico House, 6th Floor
93–99 Upper Richmond Road
Putney, London SW15 2TG
Phone: +44 (0) 20 8785 5995
Fax: +44 (0) 20 8785 5985
www.murdochbooks.co.uk

Chief Executive: Juliet Rogers
Publishing Director: Kay Scarlett

Commissioning Editor: Jane Lawson
Project Manager and Editor: Emma Hutchinson
Design Concept: Reuben Crossman
Layout: Reuben Crossman and Melanie Ngapo
Photography: Brett Stevens
Stylist: Lynsey Fryers
Production: Monique Layt
Colour separation: Colour Chiefs Pty Ltd

National Library of Australia Cataloguing-in-
  Publication Data:
Dobson, Ross, 1965-
  Fired up : no nonsense barbecuing /
  Ross Dobson.
  978 1 74196 798 2 (pbk.)
  Includes index.
  Barbecue cookery.
  641.5784

PRINTED IN CHINA 2009.

The publisher and stylist would like to thank the following companies for generously lending furniture, fabric and tableware for photography: the All Hand Made Gallery, Crowley and Grouch, Empire Vintage, Ici et La, Mokum Textiles, The Bronte Tram, Tres Fabu! and Weber.